T0345906

The Platonic Tradition

Other Books by Peter Kreeft

If Einstein Had Been a Surfer

*Philosophy 101 by Socrates:
An Introduction to Philosophy via Plato's Apology*

*Socrates Meets Descartes: The Father of Philosophy Analyzes the Father of
Modern Philosophy's Discourse on Method*

*Socrates Meets Hume: The Father of Philosophy Meets the Father
of Modern Skepticism*

*Socrates Meets Machiavelli:
The Father of Philosophy Cross-examines the Author of the Prince*

*Socrates Meets Marx: The Father of Philosophy Cross-examines the
Founder of Communism*

*Socrates Meets Kant: The Father of Philosophy Meets His Most Influential
Modern Child*

*Socrates Meets Sartre: The Father of Philosophy Cross-examines the
Founder of Existentialism*

Socrates' Children: Ancient

Socrates Children: Medieval

Socrates Children: Modern

Socrates Children: Contemporary

A Socratic Introduction to Plato's Republic

The Philosophy of Jesus

Jesus-Shock

An Ocean Full of Angels

Summa Philosophica

Socratic Logic

I Surf, Therefore I am

The Sea Within

The Platonic Tradition

Peter Kreeft

ST. AUGUSTINE'S PRESS
South Bend, Indiana

Manufactured in the United States of America

2 3 4 5 6   25 24 23 22 21

Library of Congress Cataloging in Publication Data
Names: Kreeft, Peter, author.
Title: The Platonic tradition / Peter Kreeft.
Description: South Bend, Indiana : St. Augustines Press, Inc., 2016.
Identifiers: LCCN 2016033722 | ISBN 9781587316500
(hardbound : alk. paper)
Subjects: LCSH: Plato. | Plato--Influence. | Philosophy--History.
Classification: LCC B395 .K68 2016 | DDC 184--dc23 LC
record available at https://lccn.loc.gov/2016033722

∞ The paper used in this publication meets the minimum requirements of the American National Standard for Information Sciences - Permanence of Paper for Printed Materials, ANSI Z39.48-1984.

ST. AUGUSTINE'S PRESS
www.staugustine.net

Contents

Introduction   1

Lecture I:
The Essence of the Platonic Tradition   3

Lecture II:
Socrates and Myth   19

Lecture III:
Three Additions to Plato: Aristotle, Plotinus, and Augustine   35

Lecture IV:
Christian Platonism   50

Lecture V:
Nominalism   67

Lecture VI:
Positivism   84

Lecture VII:
Nihilism   100

Lecture VIII:
Doors Out of Plato's Cave:
Signals of Transcendence in Our World   119

Introduction

This series of lectures was originally produced in audio format for Recorded Books. I have not changed its style into something more fit for eyes than for ears. It may be worth your while to imagine a voice speaking rather than a pen writing as you read these words.

It is not a work of advanced and technical "scholarship" but a bit of "philosophizing," that is, part of the loving search for wisdom. It is not designed for advanced scholars or graduate students in philosophy but for ordinary people, for "beginners."

Its purpose is not to peddle any new theory or ideology about Plato or any new explanation of Plato and Platonism, but simply to matchmake, to get you "hooked."

It treats Plato and Platonism as a single "big idea," namely what is usually called Plato's "theory of Ideas" or "theory for Forms," and therefore it only peripherally deals with the many important secondary ideas in Plato, such as the epistemology of recollection, the policies of aristocracy, or the ethics of the virtues.

And it treats this "theory of Ideas" not primarily as a theory that is justified by its power to solve logical problems or puzzles (especially what scholars call "the problem of universals") but as a vision, a "worldview." It treats this worldview as one of two, not twenty two, possible options in philosophy, the option which is perhaps best summarized by an image rather than a concept: the image of escape from the "cave" of matter, sensation, and time into another dimension, another kind of reality that is spiritual, rational, and timeless. If there is a single word for this it is probably the word "transcendence," or "moreness."

It defends this worldview or "big picture" mainly by contrast to its typically modern alternative, which can be called reductionism, positivism, materialism, nihilism, or naturalism as opposed to supernaturalism of any stripe, whether religious or not.

Finally, it argues for this worldview not so much from its premises or origins as from its conclusions or consequences (in that sense it is an example of what William James called pragmatism), especially its consequences in life, not merely in thought (in that sense it is an example of existentialism).

I trace the idea of this book back to a haunting chapter in the autobiography of a famous American philosopher who, like most philosophers, was isolated from his teenage peers by his intelligence, and spent more time in New York City's great 42nd street library than in school. One day he read Plato's *Republic*, out of idle curiosity, and when he got to the famous parable of the cave, he said: "That's me. I have to be a philosopher. I have to find my way out of the cave into the larger and greater world outside."

My hope for this book is that it may do something a little like that for you.

Lecture I:
The Essence of the Platonic Tradition

The Platonic tradition in Western philosophy is not just one of many equally central traditions. It is so much *the* central one that the very existence and survival of Western civilization depends on it. It is like the Confucian tradition in Chinese culture, or the monotheistic tradition in religion, or the human rights tradition in politics.

In the first lecture I shall define Platonism and its "big idea," the idea of a transcendent reality that the history of philosophy has labeled "Platonic Ideas" or "Platonic Forms."

In the second lecture we'll briefly explore Plato's two basic predecessors, or sources, myth and Socrates. Then we'll look at 12 applications of the Forms in Plato's own dialogs.

The third lecture will cover the three most important modifications or additions to Plato himself in the Platonic tradition: Aristotle, Plotinus, and Augustine, each of whom gave the Forms a new metaphysical address.

The fourth lecture will explore six Christian Platonists, three in the New Testament and three philosophers, Justin Martyr, Bonaventure, and Aquinas. (Surprise: Aquinas, like Aristotle, is more of a Platonist than the history book tell you.)

The next three lectures will explore the consequences of the modern abandoning of Platonism, beginning with William of Ockham's Nominalism, as the source of nearly all modern philosophical errors, and its results in the Empiricism of Locke and Hume, Kant's so-called Copernican Revolution in philosophy, and the so-called "analytic philosophy" which still dominates English and American philosophy departments.

In the sixth lecture we'll look at 12 influential kinds of Positivism or Reductionism in modern thought: in method, history, metaphysics, epistemology, ethics, sociology, politics, logic, lin-guistics, sex, psychology, and theology, exemplified by Descartes, Machiavelli, Hobbes, Marx, Kant, Mill, Comte, Rousseau, Rawls, Ayer, Derrida, Freud, Skinner, Nietzsche, and Sartre.

Lecture 7 will look at the results of abandoning the Platonic tradition in ethics—the values vacuum, or nihilism—in Ecclesi-astes, Pascal, Kierkegaard, Nietzsche, Heidegger, Sartre, Dos-toyevsky, Tolstoy, Marcel, and Buber.

In the last lecture we'll look at some experiential evidence for Platonism, doors out of the cave that are still open, signals of tran-scendence.

All this in eight short lectures? Well, yes; it's a tiny sample of an enormous and commodious storehouse, something like a wine-tasting party. It's meant to begin your thinking and reading, not end it.

A philosophy is a work of art. Every great work of art must have a central unity. That's why just about every great philoso-pher has one "big idea," one great central idea, a hub from which all other ideas radiate like spokes. For Plato this is the so-called Theory of Ideas, or Theory of Forms—though both terms are mis-leading, for they are not ideas in anyone's mind, not concepts; and they are not geometrical forms, shapes, or appearances. They are objective truths, objective realities, that are not visible to the eye of the body but only that of the mind. But the mental eye that sees them is not merely the eye of reasoning or intelligence in the narrow modern sense, but the eye of contemplation or intellectual intuition.

To call it Plato's "Theory of Forms" is misleading for a third reason: it is not a *theory* first of all but an insight, a sudden, almost mystical experience. It is mystical in the sense that it's an insight into something absolute, but it's not mystical in the sense of irra-tional. In fact it's supremely rational though not attained by rea-soning.

This single Big Idea that defines Platonism could be called the "theory of Big Ideas," because the Platonic Ideas are bigger than any ideas inside of minds, and also bigger than concrete material things outside of minds. They're "bigger than both of us," bigger or more real than either concepts or things. They are the standards or patterns for all concepts and all things, and they account for the unity of concepts and things. For instance, our ideas of justice, or squareness, or humanness can correspond to just things, or square things, or human things only because both our ideas and those things participate in the same Platonic Form.

This Big Idea of Plato's is most famously expressed in the *Republic*, the most famous book in the history of philosophy. Things become famous, and remembered, because they are loved, and the *Republic* is loved not for its politics, much of which are absurd, but for its psychology (the world's first, by the way), and above all for one short passage, the most famous passage in the entire history of philosophy, the parable of the cave, in which Plato invites us to come with him out of our small, comfortable, conventional little shadowland into a startlingly larger world outside this cave, and see the realities *of* which these shadows are shadows. When we do that, we will at first certainly be confused and blink when we see this sunlight. The reaction of my students to Plato's Theory of Ideas is typically that of Horatio to Hamlet when he first sees the ghost he did not previously believe in. While Horatio is in this amazed state of mind, Hamlet says to him, "There are more things in heaven and earth, Horatio, than are dreamt of in your philosophy." That is the essential point of Platonism: moreness, transcendence, another *kind* of reality outside our cave.

The tendency of typically modern thought is just the opposite: reductionism, demythologization, debunking; that there are *fewer* things in heaven and earth, that is, in objective reality, than in our philosophies. That's the modern tendency: to contract, to reduce. And the reason for this is very clear. For only when we reduce the complex to the simple and the mysterious to the clear can we comprehend it scientifically and conquer it technologically. That's our essential modern project, our main claim to fame, our great success story. Plato's project is the opposite: not to conquer things by making them smaller but to let *ourselves* be conquered by something greater. Modern scientific truths are like poker chips with which we can calculate and win. Our mind encloses such truths, and uses them. They work very well. But Plato's truth is like a cathedral which makes us humbly bow to enter. It encloses us. But we become taller when we bow, for we feel we are in a larger world when we are in a cathedral, or in Plato's philosophy. The Platonic Ideas are not in our mind; we are in them. They are not our servants; they are our masters. That's why we experience awe and wonder at them. Most philosophies don't have that power over our souls.

When we speak of awe and wonder we don't usually think of modern philosophers. But I've described only the psychological effect of the idea that I've labeled the heart of Platonism. Can we be a little more specific about what it means?

We can define it in three different ways: either very broadly, or very narrowly, or between these two extremes.

Very broadly, it means what the Greeks called *Logos* and what we might translate as *order*: that reality has an internal order, an intelligibility, a system—that it makes sense. That order is not just our invention—our mind's imposing structure and meaning—but rather is really there, in everything. It's discovered rather than invented.

Things are ordered because they have intelligible natures or essences. The primary question "What is it?" has real answers. Reality is intelligible to mind. Being is open to reason and reason is open to being.

We can also define it more narrowly, as most history of philosophy texts do: it means that there are always universals as well as particulars; that redness and holiness and chair-ness are real just as red things and holy things and chairs are real. It means that adjectives are real just as nouns are; that when two or more things have the same quality, that quality is as real as the things, and (according to Plato) in fact is real independent of those things. Therefore, if all holy men perished, holiness would still be and would still be holiness; and if all red things in the universe perished, redness would still be, though it would not be anywhere in the universe.

A third definition of Plato's Theory of Forms is that visible, concrete, particular things are *images* or reflections of their forms, or essences, or Platonic Ideas; they are like them, or analogous to them; that the whole material world that we see here in our cave is a series of shadows of more real immaterial things. We live in the Shadowlands. (That was the title of the C. S. Lewis movie: a perfect title, because that Platonic insight was Lewis's essential philosophy.) The whole world we see is an image of a world we do not see, as a painting is an image of something in the painter's mind. When we see a painting, our mind forms an image of it, but the painting itself is an image of an idea in the painter's mind. The easiest way to understand this is to think of the painter as God and the painting as the world, so that the whole material universe is a work of art and our understanding of the Ideas it reflects is a kind of mental telepathy with the Mind of the Artist.

I've used the language of religion because that makes Platonism clearer, even though Platonism is not religion. Plato, like Socrates, was a monotheist but he was quite agnostic about the divine mind, and he nowhere says that it is a divine *person; that* identification was a step made later by Christian Platonists. That goes beyond Plato, but not necessarily against him.

There are three critical differences between the physical world and the world of the Forms. This higher world, or realm, or dimension, is eternal while the world of concrete things is temporal and changing. Living things like trees or round things like bubbles or just things like societies come into being and pass away, but life and roundness and justice do not. A second difference is that living or round or just things are many, while life is one and roundness is one and justice is one. A third difference is that life and roundness and justice are perfect, perfectly round or perfectly just, while all life is infected with death, and round bubbles are always a little bumpy instead of perfect spheres, and just societies are always mixed with some injustice.

C. S. Lewis explains Platonism in *The Allegory of Love* by calling its worldview "symbolism" and contrasting it to allegory. He writes:

"It is of the very nature of thought and language to represent what is immaterial in picturable terms. What is good or happy has always been high like the heavens and bright like the sun. Evil and misery were deep and dark from the first. . . . To ask how these married pairs of sensibles and insensibles first came together would be great folly; the real question is how they ever came apart. . . . This fundamental equivalence between the immaterial and the material may be used by the mind in two ways...On the one hand you can start with an immaterial fact, such as the passions which you actually experience, and can then invent visibilia to express them. . . . This is allegory. . . . But there is another way of using the equivalence, which is almost the opposite of allegory, and which I could call sacramentalism or symbolism. If our passions, being immaterial, can be copied by material inventions, then it is possible that our material world in turn is the copy of an invisible world, of something else. The attempt to read that something else through its sensible imitations, to see the archetype in the copy, is what I mean by symbolism or sacramentalism. . . . The allegorist leaves the given— his own passions—to talk of that which is confessedly less real. . . a fiction. The symbolist leaves the given (the material world) to find that which is more real. Symbolism comes to us from Greece. It makes its first appearance. . . with the dialogs of Plato. The Sun is the copy of the Good. Time is the moving image of eternity. All visible things exist just insofar as they succeed in imitating the Forms."

Plato's Theory of Forms is the central doctrine of the *Republic*. The *Republic* is usually classified as a book about politics. But Plato clearly says in the *Republic* that he is going to deal with politics only as an analogy, a parallel or illustration, for morality, for ethics. He wants to see the morally good man and the good life more clearly by looking at the good society, because that is bigger and easier to see. Politics is only the *Republic's* means; ethics is its end.

And the most fundamental differences between two philosophical positions in ethics, and also in politics, are always rooted in fundamental differences in metaphysics, which is the division of philosophy that deals with the nature of reality. Ethics and politics deal with the *good*, private and public; and metaphysics deals with the *real*; but goodness and reality cannot be separated. The *ought* depends on the *is*. Values depend on facts, on truth.

Let me put the same point in another way. You can answer the ethical question—What should we be and do, individually and socially? What is the good life and the good society?—only if you answer the prior anthropological question—What is a human being? Is humanity merely a lucky cosmic accident, a fortunate arrangement of molecules, a chemical equation, an evolved slime pool, an animal which has learned to wear clothes? Is Mind merely Brain? Or—the opposite extreme—is man really God in disguise? Or at least a god or an angel? Or is man a double thing, half beast, half angel? Or is he something between beast and angel? But you can answer this anthropological question— What is man?—only if you answer the prior metaphysical question—What is? What is real? What is reality? If spirit does not exist, we cannot be god or angel or any kind of spirit; while if matter does not exist, that's the only thing we *could* be. And involved in all four of these questions—the question of metaphysics and anthropology and ethics and politics—is also the question of epistemology—How can we know?

Let me put the point in still another way—the point about ethics depending on metaphysics. When you read the *Republic*, you probably wish you could ask this question of Plato: Your picture of the good life in the *Republic*, both the good society and the good individual, may be a beautiful and noble ideal, Plato, but is it *real*? There never has been a perfectly good, perfectly just state or a perfectly good, perfectly just individual, so isn't your ideal just that, *your* ideal? Your personal opinion, subjective? In your mind, and maybe in mine too, but is it *real*? Does anything more than Plato justify Plato? Aren't your so-called Platonic Ideas (such as the Justice you define in the *Republic*) merely *your* ideas? How can they be part of the real world?

The typically modern view is that the real world is merely the world we can see and touch, the world we can know best by science—that's the objective world—and that there's also a subjective world—an inner world of our private, personal thoughts and opinions and feelings, which we change as often as we change our underwear. So there are two worlds, the world without and the world within: the world of objective things we can have opinions and desires about, and the world of those subjective opinions and desires. Both of these two worlds *change*. Both worlds are imperfect. They get better or worse; they are never perfect.

If this typically modern metaphysics is true, then what follows for ethics? There are then only two places for the good to be: in the objective world of rocks or the subjective world of opinions and feelings. And since values aren't things like rocks, which we discover, they must be subjective opinions or feelings. Ethics becomes merely "values" that we posit, that we make. Values are not like rocks; we don't discover them. They're like art: we create them, both individually and socially, collectively, or culturally.

But Plato thinks values *are* things like rocks. They're objectively real. In fact, they're harder than rocks, more real than rocks, more unchangeable, more unyielding than rocks. We don't see them with the eyes of the body but with the eyes of the mind. But they're not *in* the mind any more than rocks are in the eye.

This fundamental metaphysical difference between Plato and modernity is the root of a fundamental ethical difference. In the typically modern view, Plato is an unrealistic dreamer and Thrasymachus the Sophist is right when he defines justice as simply the label pinned on the laws by whoever has the power to make them. So justice is ultimately power, as Thrasymachus argues in the *Republic* and Machiavelli, much later, in *The Prince*. Even if you prefer a less violent and freer and more democratic definition of justice as the consensus of free citizens rather than raw power, it's still metaphysically in the same position: it's only subjective and man-made. It may be *good* but it's not *true*.

Plato wants to expand that narrow world, that cave of ours— (a) in metaphysics, by showing us a different kind of reality outside the cave; and (b) in epistemology, by showing us a different kind of knowing than cave-knowing, a knowing he calls wisdom; and (c) in anthropology, by showing us our new identity, our hidden soul-power to transcend the cave; and (d) in ethics, by showing us another kind of good, a good and goal and end and destiny that transcends the cave. Plato isn't creating this new world, like a fantasy writer; he's describing it, like Columbus describing America. Plato isn't expanding the real world, he's showing us that we've contracted it by creeping into our cave.

Platonism isn't comfortable. If we follow his lead and emerge from the cave, it may look to us at first like a contraction of the world, because we will lose something: control. We will stand blinking and confused in the sun. And there is a second danger: when we eventually stop blinking and learn to see in the sunlight and come to know this greater world, we may then denigrate the lower world, for we will know that this lower cave world is only a shadow, an image, of the greater, better, higher world. But it is a real image and a precious image, because of what it is an image of, so this danger can and should be avoided.

You can take two attitudes to an image, once you realize it's only an image. You can say: "It's only an image, not the real thing, so out with it." Or you can say, "That's an image of something great and precious, so that makes it a precious image," like a photo of your beloved.

There is another typically modern objection to Plato's invitation to go with him on his journey out of the cave, and many of you are probably thinking this objection right now. It comes down to this: Even if you choose to follow Plato, isn't the choice as subjective as your taste in art or music? Plato offers us two options, two philosophies: cave light or sunlight. We must choose. But we may argue that the fact that we must *choose* between these two philosophies means that philosophy is only in our minds. We may think that the choice between believing that the world outside the cave is only subjective or believing that it is objective is *itself* only subjective, only what I happen to like, or what my society or my religion or my philosophy teacher or my genetics and brain chemistry has caused me to believe, rather than something as real as a rock.

But if that's true—if our choice is purely our subjective preference and not objectively right or wrong, true or false; if it is not decided by reason but by some other force in nature or nurture, heredity or environment; if my rational intelligence is merely an effect of irrational matter plus irrational desires, as Freud says— in that case, there's no *real reason* why I *should* believe any one idea rather than any other, including that idea! For if there are only causes, not reasons; if the material forces in the cave and the subjective forces inside my own mind are the only things that determine any of my ideas; if there are no Platonic Ideas but only *my* ideas—then no idea I have can ever be known to be either true or false, any more than the pistons in your car engine are either true or false, or the row of dominos that cause each other to fall are either true or false. It's just the way the thing happens to work. There are only causes, not reasons. My psyche just happens to work that way. But if there's no spiritual designer and programmer behind my computer brain, why should I trust that computer? If Mind is only subjective and Reason is only the way my brain happens to work, why should I think the computer or its software corresponds to reality?

Freud is a good example of the anti-Platonist on this issue, the issue of the authority of Reason, which is the vehicle that takes us out of the cave. Freud says, on the last page of his most philosophical work, *Civilization and Its Discontents*, that the one and only thing he is certain of is that all our reasoning is only rationalizing of our desires. It seems to me that that's the only sentence in the book that we can be absolutely certain is false, because it's self-contradictory. Because if that's true, then that piece of reasoning too is only rationalizing, so why should I believe it, if it's only Freud himself rationalizing his own desires? Why should I let

Freud's desires determine *my beliefs*? If reason is only subjective, then that piece of reason is only subjective too: it's only subjective that it's only subjective. It refutes itself. It commits rational suicide.

So Reason must be in touch with objective truth, at least sometimes. If it weren't, then we could have no standard for judging when it wasn't. If there's no real money, we have no right to judge that any money is counterfeit. If there's no ultimate truth, we can't judge any thought as erroneous. So some kind of thought, some kind of reason, *must* get outside the cave. Plato *must* be right about that.

That's just a logical argument, an abstract one. Here's another argument, a much more concrete and experiential one, for believing that Plato is right and there is a world of eternal, objective, universal, truths outside the cave of our sensations and opinions and their material objects. The argument is simply that we experience it! Our minds bump up against the objective and unchangeable reality of $2 + 2 = 4$, or "triangles always have 180 degrees," or "justice is a virtue," or "effects must have causes." Our bodies bump up against real physical walls that we can't walk through, and our minds just as really and truly and unarguably bump up against real walls of thought that it's simply impossible to knock down or change. Triangles and virtues are no less real than physical walls and rocks. If the truths of mathematics and metaphysics were merely mental, if we made them up, then we could change them, as we can change unicorns or mermaids or hobbits. But we can't. And the same is true of the laws of ethics. If justice were simply man-made, we could change it just as we can change traffic laws. But we can't. We can't make genocide right or honesty wrong. We discover them; we don't invent them. And where do we discover them? Where are they? In the world outside the cave. ("World" here does not mean "material world" or "planet," just "some kind of ordered reality.")

This gives us a radically different anthropology. "Know thyself" was the first commandment of the god of the Delphic Oracle; and like Socrates, Plato took that commandment seriously. He defined man as a rational animal. Reason is what distinguishes man from the beasts.

But what is reason? The typically modern answer is simply calculation, cleverness. Plato's answer is wisdom, understanding, insight into the Forms. In the *Republic* he summarizes four levels of reason, parallel to four levels of reality, in a geometrical figure that he calls a divided line, a line divided into four unequal parts.

The first and lowest level of knowledge is mere secondhand opinions based on reflections or images or secondhand reports of real things.

The next level is direct sense experience. Plato calls this belief, because we believe or assume that our senses show us reality, but we don't prove it. And the level of reality that is the object of sensory belief is actual material objects.

A third level is logical and mathematical reasoning, and its object is logical and mathematical truths, like the truths of geometry. These are quantitative, not qualitative; and they are hypothetical, they depend on other truths, as in logic all conclusions depend on their premises. Logic is "if. . . then. . . " reasoning.

The fourth and highest level is knowledge of the Forms. This knowledge is not mere appearance, or belief, or hypothetical reasoning, but direct insight into an unchangeable qualitative Form like Justice or Beauty or Human Nature or Life. This knowledge is what makes man human, distinguishing us from both beasts and computers. Beasts have senses that are often better than ours, and computers can do reasoning much more accurately and quickly than we can. So how are we more than apes with cameras and computers—animals with enhanced sensory powers (which is level two) and reasoning powers (which is level three)? What can we do that neither animals nor computers can do? We can understand eternal, necessary truths. We can know the essential Natures of things. That's what it is to get out of the cave.

Plato thus invites us into the discovery of a whole new world, a third world in addition to the world of matter and the world of subjective minds and ideas: a world of objective Ideas, Forms, Essences, the eternally real and unchangeable Natures of Things.

And this third world alone unifies the other two worlds, because both reflect the same Forms. Why can I know that balls are round? Because both the ball and my mind's concept participate in the same Form of Roundness. Why is my subjective judgment that 2 + 2 = 4 true of real rabbits and rocks? Because both my judgments and the rabbits and rocks reflect the same Forms, and the same relationships between the forms of 2 and 4. My geometry can measure pyramids because both reflect the same Form of Triangularity. Because there is the same red both in the rose and in my sense perception, I can see the rose as red. But what is redness? It's not a rose, and it's not a perception; it's what I perceive in the rose. But the rose is only red; it's not redness. The rose only HAS redness. Some redness, not all of it. That's why other things can also be red. But other *colors* can't be red. Colors themselves are Forms.

We can know all three worlds: we can know the Forms as well as things in the world and opinions and sensations in our minds. Why? Why can I know objective truths that go beyond the senses, beyond red roses and round balls and two rabbits? Why can I know facts like these, that justice is a virtue and that wholes are greater than parts and that nothing exists without a reason and that effects need causes? Because my mind is somehow in touch with the world of eternal Forms, with a light from outside the cave. Ideas like truth and goodness and beauty are produced *in* my mind—but not *by* my mind but by the impact of something on my mind, something that's like a meteor coming down from outer space, or like an angel coming down Jacob's ladder from Heaven. It doesn't come from the earth, because it's not made of matter, and it doesn't come from my mind. It comes *to* my mind and judges my mind as right or wrong depending on whether my mind reflects it and conforms to it or not.

What kind of mind, what kind of consciousness, knows the Forms? Platonism gives us an expanded epistemology, or theory of knowledge, as well as an expanded metaphysics, or theory of being. To see this, let's distinguish five kinds of knowing. All five begin with a kind of wonder.

The first is ordinary, unreflective, undisciplined knowing, sense perception and common sense. Its wonder is simple factual curiosity. Basically, that's the first two levels of Plato's Divided Line. The other four try in different ways to rise above this and improve it.

The second is scientific knowing, in the modern sense. It uses proof by empirical testing and mathematical measurement, and its end is technological power over nature. The standard for scientific hypotheses is; do they *work*? Its wonder is: "I wonder what will work to give me the most power, power of theoretical ideas and power of practical technology." This wonder ends when the knowledge comes.

The third is philosophical knowledge of reasons and causes by logical reasoning, getting to the kind of thing Aristotle and Plato both got to. Philosophy, like science, begins in wonder, according to the Greeks, but in science the wonder ends when the knowledge comes. The difference between science and philosophy is that it's much harder to come to the end in philosophy.

The fourth kind of knowing is the contemplation of the truth for its own sake, and the wonder that begins this is contemplative wonder. This kind of knowledge ends in wonder as well as beginning in wonder. It is a sophisticated version of the contemplative wonder of a little child.

The fifth kind of knowledge is mystical. The myths suggest it, and Plato ends his most important dialogs with myths because nothing else can suggest it better. It is an active, actual experience of the ultimate, something like "knowledge" in the Biblical sense, which meant sexual intercourse. It's a kind of ecstatic play: ecstatic because you are out of yourself, out of self-consciousness, out of your ordinary mind, out of control, in a kind of intellectual orgasm. And it's play because it has no practical end beyond itself; it *is* our end. (That's true of contemplation too, but contemplation is *intellectual*, not mystical.) Plato strongly suggests, in many places, like his *Seventh Letter* and the *Phaedrus* and the *Symposium* and in what he says about the Absolute Good in the *Republic*, that this mystical knowledge, which cannot be put into words, is the whole point of philosophy and, indeed, of human life itself.

In addition to these expanded levels in metaphysics and epistemology, Platonism also gives us an expanded ethics or life-view, or practice, as well as an expanded world-view, or theory. The ethical consequence of Platonic Forms can hardly be exaggerated. Because for the ancients ethics is fundamentally about something much more than laws and rights and duties. It's first of all about the most important question you can ask: what is the end of man, the meaning of life, the *summum bonum*, the greatest good, the purpose of our existence? What ought I to be and do?

The answer to this question depends on metaphysics. If nature is the final reality, if matter and human minds are all that exists, then my meaning and end is here, in this world: the satisfaction of merely temporal needs. If, on the other hand, I know a reality greater than nature, then I can aspire to some sort of union with that, even in this life, and I can hope for a more perfect union with it after death. And even in this life, if I have some kind of participation in the supreme good that transcends time, then I can take that as my standard. I can hitch my wagon to a star and navigate the seas of time with my head in the clouds even as my feet are on the ground or on the deck of the boat. If I can know the Absolute Good, I can judge relative goods by that standard, including my own soul, and also my society. That's why Plato wants philosophers to become kings: because the philosopher is not merely the clever scholar but the wise sage who knows Perfect Justice and therefore can judge among imperfect justices, among the shadows in the cave, by the light he has seen outside the cave.

Thus Plato would argue that only a Platonist, or a supernaturalist, or an idealist, or a transcendentalist—whichever label you want to use—only he can justify radical rebellion, because only he can judge existing society by a higher standard, as the Jewish prophets did. He can let the Good judge us instead of judging it. How could it judge us if it's only our fabrication? How can I impose *my* ideas, or *our* ideas, on you? I can't. But perhaps *my* ideas and yours can alike be judged by *the* Ideas. If not, if we can't "let God be God," then one of us has to play God to the other, or else just be indifferent and skeptical and never go beyond "tolerance." Theologically put, the alternatives to Platonism are idolatry or not giving a damn. Politically put, the alternatives to Platonism are tyranny (or totalitarianism or terrorism) or else anarchy ("what the hell?"). So you see no philosopher is more relevant to our contemporary world than old Plato.

Lecture II:
Socrates and Myth

No philosophical theory ever just happens. In fact, nothing ever just happens; everything that begins has causes. And even though the primary cause of a philosophy is the mind of the philosopher, which is something spiritual and inward and personal, there are always external causes too. The philosopher's influences and predecessors act as catalysts in the spiritual chemistry of the reaction that takes place in the philosopher's mind; or, to change the analogy, they act like food—food for thought.

There were two main catalysts for Plato's "Big Idea," Plato's theory of Forms, in his social, historical background: ancient myth and Socrates's logic. These two seemed as opposite as any two things could possibly be, but they both combined to lead Plato to the same insight.

The word "myth" means, literally, "sacred story." Myth does not necessarily mean something false (except to a cynic and skeptic) but something that claims to teach a truth in symbols. Symbolic thinking is very close to Platonic philosophy, as C. S. Lewis explained in that long quotation in Lecture I about symbolism and allegory.

When I speak of mythic thinking, I mean both the thinking that *makes* the myths in the first place and the thinking that hears them and enjoys them. The essence of all mythic thinking is in one way very different than Platonic thinking, because it is concrete rather than abstract, stories about divine or semidivine heroes rather than definitions of universal Ideas. But in another way myth is very similar to Platonic philosophy in that these heroes are archetypes, superhuman models for the persons and events in the lower world that imitate them and are images of them, as Platonic Forms are archetypes for things and events that are images of them in the world of matter and appearance. Each archetype is *one perfect* model for *many imperfect* imitations, or images. Both in the myths and in Plato's philosophy the archetypes have an exalted quality, a perfection; they are paradigms, and they have an authority over human lives, which imitate them.

The gods' role as archetypes is exalted in two ways: in time and space. They are exalted in time by being put into the sacred *past*, when the gods were on earth or closer to the earth; and they are exalted in space by being put into the heavens, at the top of the cosmic totem pole while we mortals are somewhere near the middle. (By the way, 'all' premodern thinking sees the cosmos as a hierarchy.) Huston Smith, describing primitive religions, says that

> what is probably the most important single feature of primal spirituality is its symbolist mentality. The symbolist vision sees the things of the world as transparent to their divine source. Human ancestors are viewed as prolongations of the tribe's earliest ancestors, who were divine. This makes them the bridge that connects the current generation with its first and supreme ancestor.

The "first and supreme ancestor" is the archetype.

Thoroughly materialistic minds—minds that cannot even imagine anyone believing in a reality that is both spiritual and supernatural—almost always interpret myth as primitive science. For instance, Apollo, the sun god, is to them only a primitive symbol for the sun. In fact it was exactly the opposite: the sun was a symbol for Apollo. Jupiter was not a crude, primitive way of referring to thunder; thunder was his rage. Neptune was not a prescientific version of sodium chloride suspended in two parts of hydrogen plus one part of oxygen. Why would they camouflage the fact that there's a lot of salt water out there by talking about a very large invisible man with windy breath? Neptune was not a symbol of the sea; the sea was a symbol of Neptune. Primitives were much more interested in gods than in gases, because they were more interested in persons than in things. And that made them not nearly as primitive as many modern scientific thinkers who are more interested in things than persons, and who reduce even persons to things, like gases and genes.

This symbolism involves hierarchy—eternal archetypes are superior to their earthly examples—and this is a very un-modern notion. Science knows hierarchy too, but only a quantitative and material hierarchy, a hierarchy only of size, where the macrocosm, or larger world, is simply thirteen or fourteen billion years long and billions of galaxies wide, and the microcosm, the smaller world, is simply the particles of matter and energy that combine to make the visible world. At most, science admits only a hierarchy of complexity: human brains are more complex than stars. But complexity is still a quantitative notion. You have to quantify something before it becomes an object of strictly scientific thinking. But the hierarchy of Platonic thinking is a qualitative hierarchy, a hierarchy of value, with the absolute ruling principle being the Good. The only values science can deal with are quantitative values, like the value of atomic weight, or money. The Platonic Forms are *ontologically* better, *metaphysically* more, more real, more authentic, than the physical things that exemplify them, as you are more real than photographs of you. As one photo is more authentic than another, one person is more human than another, more or less a real man or a real woman, but neither of them is Perfect Humanity Itself.

The typically modern mind believes that these archetypes, these qualitative Forms which we use as our standards of value measurement, are inventions of our mind. Platonic thought says they are as real as rocks.

There are only two options. When it comes to values and qualities—as distinct from just scientific, material quantities—either the truth is objective or subjective. Either we find these things or we make them. When we think of things like justice or beauty or virtue or goodness or life or soul, our minds either enter into something greater than ourselves and conform to it, or we create it, as we invent languages and social systems and laws. The latter is the typically modern option. Myth is the earliest pre-philosophical form of the alternative option. Platonism is the earliest philosophical form of it. Aristotelianism is only an adjusted form of Platonism, as we shall see in the next lecture. Whether the superior truth we conform to is a mythical god, a Platonic Idea, or an Aristotelian Form, all three are versions of a hierarchical worldview, a cosmic order, a larger-than-life meaning and purpose and intelligibility and truth and rationality that we discover and believe and know and live, and conform to and find our authentic selves in by that conformity. Or else, in the alternative philosophy, which is more typically modern, it is we who make all reason, order, meaning, and purpose, except in science. In the typically modern worldview, the scientific method is the only way to find objective truth, and all this Platonic stuff is only myth—"myth" in the new, modern sense of something fictitious.

Platonism is a philosophy, not a religion, but it's most easily understood by a religious parallel: the two options are that either God created us in His own image, or we created Him in ours. Either He wrote the play we are in, or we are writing it; either we are only the players or also the authors. Thus the title of the old Paul Newman pro-euthanasia movie is exactly right: "Whose life is it, anyway?" That second, modern option, judged by the religious standpoint, is the basic violation of the very first commandment: "Thou shalt have no other gods before Me," the commandment against idolatry. And the primary idolatry would be to worship ourselves. One psychologist, Paul Vitz, says America is the most polytheistic nation in history because we worship not one thousand gods or ten thousand gods but three hundred fifty million gods.

In the *Republic* Plato severely criticized the Homeric myths that were the official state religion of ancient Athens, because he admired and agreed with his teacher, Socrates, who had been tried and executed as an atheist because he could not honestly confess that he believed in these gods as the state believed in them. But neither Socrates nor Plato were atheists; they were pious agnostic monotheists. They were agnostic about their myths because the myths, and the gods of the myths, were irrational. When Socrates speaks of the gods, he's not serious, but when he speaks of "the god" in the singular, he is. The gods have in the plural, names; "the god" is nameless. The Unknown God that some Athenians were still worshipping four hundred fifty years later, when St. Paul visited Athens, was the god Socrates worshipped, and the only one that Paul, like Socrates, approved of.

In Plato's dialog the *Euthyphro*, Socrates asks Euthyphro the crucial question: is a thing good merely because the gods love it, or do they love it because it is good? Euthyphro thinks the first. His gods are the willful, arbitrary, irrational tyrants of Greek mythology. Socrates thinks it's the second option, that his god is rational and moral, and wills only good. And that is all that Socrates claims to know about him. In Socrates, the sun of reason has risen and dispelled the fogs of myth. Socrates, more than any other single person in history, invented the new way of thinking that we call reason, or rather he is the first who sharply separated and distinguished it from mythical thinking. Instead of relying on blind feelings and blind faith in the stories of Homer, which both rose from and appealed to the unconscious imagination, Socrates demanded conscious reasons, definitions, and arguments. Socrates was the first person who clearly knew what a logical argument was. A few decades later, Aristotle based the world's first logic textbook on crates's lived example.

How did Socrates's logic contribute to Plato's big idea, the theory of Forms? In this way: An argument proves its conclusion only if it passes three check point: If its terms are clear, its premises true, and its logic valid, that is, the conclusion logically follows from the premises. The first thing—defining terms—is what takes up most of the space in Plato's Socratic dialogs: finding out what our terms mean, making them clear. But how shall we do that? The answer is by definition.

A definition expresses the universal and necessary and unchangeable essence of the thing defined, unlike concrete examples which only express what is particular and accidental and changeable. For instance, you cannot define a man as a Greek, or as an adult, or as somebody who looks like Plato, even though Greeks and adults and people who look like Plato are indeed men. You must define man by omitting all the changeable and particular features and find the universal essence. Man is essentially a rational animal, a living organism with a soul capable of reason. That is his essence. A definition always seeks the essence of a thing. If there really are no essences, there can be no real definitions but only nominal definitions, that is, only reports about how we have conventionally agreed to use words.

Each Socratic dialog searches for an essence. That's why Socrates always asks the question, WHAT IS *x?* And since Socrates was a very practical man who knew he had only one lifetime to spend, he concentrated on the most important things to define, which were almost always moral virtues. In the *Laches* he asks, what is courage? The *Lysis* he asks, what is friendship? The *Meno* he asks, what is teaching? The *Republic* he asks, what is justice? The *what* is the essence, as distinct from the appearances or the particular examples, the instances.

These definitions that Socrates sought are not just nominal definitions, definitions of names, conventions of usage, decisions about how to use words. They are real definitions, definitions of real essences, the essences of real things. They are either right or wrong, true or false. They're not decisions of will about how we want to use words, but acts of understanding, intellectual insights into the real natures of things.

In other words, Socrates always is looking for some Platonic Form. All Plato did in his theory of Forms was to explain what Socrates was doing, to erect a metaphysical foundation under Socrates's logical quest.

So both the irrational myths and the demythologized reasoning of Socrates contributed to the same Platonic Theory of Forms. The Forms are both archetypes and definitions. They function as archetypes when expressed concretely in mythic symbols, and they function as definitions when expressed abstractly in logical arguments.

Every one of Plato's 30 dialogs centers on a Form, a "what." I'll summarize each of them but I want to spend most of our time on the *Apology of Socrates*, Plato's paean of praise to his master. This is perhaps the greatest secular speech in the history of Western civilization. It is a defense not only of Socrates but also of the life of philosophy that he is being martyred for, and a defense of the kind of human being and human life which is exemplified most perfectly by Socrates. The very last line of the *Apology* says that Socrates was "of all men then living, of all we ever met, the best, the wisest, and the most just."

At the heart of the *Apology* we find a riddling reference to an implied but not expressed definition of that Platonic Form that is in one way the primary one: the self. What is the essence of the self? "Know thyself" was the first commandment of the god of the Delphic oracle who inspired Socrates to become a philosopher. And now Socrates reveals that he has solved the oracle's riddle. But he does this in a riddling way, indirectly, not directly. Watch how clever he is.

His deepest conviction—expressed twice in the *Apology* with the warning words, "You will laugh and jeer at this, but please listen," because it sounds so outrageous—is that "no evil can ever possibly happen to a good man, in this world or the next." Socrates claims to be *certain* of this apparently-ridiculous thing. Socrates doubts and questions everything, even commonsense platitudes—he is almost a skeptic—and he claims to be certain of just a very few things, but each one of them is an outrageous paradox, a deep surprise. For instance, he knows that evil is only ignorance, and that learning is really remembering. And the certainty he expresses in the *Apology*, that no evil can ever happen to a good man, is the most important certainty of all. It can change your life. It means that there is only one thing necessary: being good; and if you are, then no evil can ever happen to you. What justifies this conviction? It seems absurd, because evil is happening to a good man right now, even as Socrates is saying that it can't; for he is about to be unjustly executed precisely because he is good and cannot honestly profess a faith in the wicked gods of the state. Why is Socrates certain that that very situation that he is in is *not* what it seems to be, that that's not evil happening to a good man?

The answer is that Socrates has discovered the essence of a man. He has solved the riddle of the oracle, "Know thyself." Your self is your soul, your inner self, your personality, your character. That is Socrates's implicit answer to *"know thyself,"* the great puzzle written over the door of the temple of the Delphic oracle, the only Greek god Socrates ever took seriously. This oracle gave Socrates his philosophical vocation by declaring (to Socrates's friend) that no one in the world was wiser than Socrates, which made Socrates puzzle over this riddle because he knew he had no wisdom at all. The puzzle was a beautiful irony because the oracle was using the Socratic method of questioning—riddling, rather than answering—to teach Socrates to use the Socratic method of questioning to unravel the riddle. Socrates went around trying to find a wise man by questioning supposedly wise men, so that he finally discovered what wisdom was: knowing that you had no wisdom, that only God had wisdom.

This made Socrates a philosopher, in fact the first, greatest, and archetypal philosopher, the grandfather of all other philosophers, beginning with Plato. And now, in his swan song, the *Apology*, Socrates shows, indirectly, that he has found the answer to the oracle's primary riddle, *know thyself*. "My" self is my soul, and therefore no other man, but only I, can make myself good or evil, wise or foolish, virtuous or vicious. So no evil can just *happen* to me. No other man can harm my soul, only my body. If he kills me unjustly, he harms only his own soul, not mine.

The self was the first Platonic Form that Socrates discovered: the form of himself, the *essential* self.

We could go so far as to say that it was Socrates who for the first time clearly discovered the soul, the psyche. Before Socrates, the Greek word *psyche* meant ghost, the *less* real, less solid, less human image that survived the death of the body, as a ghost image sometimes flickers for a second on a TV screen after you turn it off. But for Socrates the body is the image of the soul, not vice versa! When Socrates announced that the essence of the self was the soul, his contemporaries must have thought he was crazy, because he seemed to them to be saying that your true self is your ghost.

Unfortunately, most of us are still primitive pre-Socratic thinkers when we think of the soul, for when our movies show the soul departing from the body at death, it's always a ghost, a cloud, something insubstantial. If Socrates made a movie about death he'd show the *body* as a cloud, a rainbow, a short-lived, barely-substantial thing, and the soul would look like a bar of iron. The body is part of me only because it is the home of the soul, for a little while. For after I die, my corpse is no longer me, but my soul is.

This is the first Platonic Form to be discovered, the most important one, for if you don't know yourself, then you don't know who it is that knows anything else!

Socrates was probably the second most influential person in the history of Western civilization, next to Jesus. For what distinguishes Western civilization above all is respect for reason and rational morality, and these stem from Socrates more than anyone else. Even modern science, which has changed our lives so radically, stems historically from philosophy—each of the sciences came to develop its own method and independence from philosophy, like children moving away from home; and the father of all philosophy is Socrates.

Renaissance humanists regularly cited Socrates as the primary example of the righteous pagan. Aquinas called him the greatest of philosophers. In explaining why Socrates never wrote anything, Aquinas said that, like Christ, Socrates had no need to teach by writing because his teaching was of a higher order. Socrates is philosophy's Christ: all other philosophers depend on him, through Plato, who is like his intellectual missionary and evangelist, sort of like a Matthew, Mark, Luke, John, and Paul all rolled into one.

The *way* the dialogs show us what a thing is, is not simply by a verbal definition announced at the end of a process of merely logical analysis. A Platonic dialog is a wonderfully complex, multi-layered thing, always with a deep psychological dimension, each character representing something in the soul of all of us. Each dialog has a dramatic human interaction as well as a logical one, as a double way to see the Form it is looking for–the first concrete and personal, the second abstract and logical. Plato began his career as a poet and dramatist. Though he publicly burned the dramas he had written when he met Socrates, to dramatize his conversion to philosophy, fortunately he did not and could not burn the dramatist in his heart.

Sometimes the drama of a dialog ends with the discovery of the Form they seek (as in the *Republic*) and sometimes it doesn't (as in the *Meno*). But even when they don't succeed, they do in a sense, for they find what it isn't, which is like finding the negative photographic image of it. Finding what it's not is a stage toward finding what it is, because we always begin by confusing what it is with some things that it's not, and we have to be dispossessed of this garbage before we can eat the right food. Socrates is more often our garbage man than our chef. Readers are often frustrated by Socrates because after pages of argument he doesn't come to a positive conclusion. But you shouldn't be frustrated by that— not because he's trying to make you a skeptic, but because he's trying to make you a philosopher. He *could* cook your mental food, but he won't. He cleans your mental kitchen so you can do your own cooking.

We're never allowed to be passive with Socrates and let him feed us, like baby birds passively letting mama bird put worms in their mouths. We have to hunt. He invites us on a hunting expedition. And even in the later dialogs of Plato, written long after Socrates died, when the living example of Socrates recedes and the dialogs have less personal drama and more positive philosophical conclusions, they always remain dialogs, *dramas* of ideas, unpredictable journeys.

What we are looking for in these journeys is always a universal. The special sciences also seek universal formulas, like $E = mc^2$, but this is still partial, not universal knowledge. Physics is not biology and biology is not math. But philosophy (especially metaphysics) is the study of everything. In the *Republic*, Plato defines the distinctiveness of the philosopher this way: the philosopher is the one who seeks the whole of beauty, or justice, or wisdom, or whatever the Form it is that he's seeking, rather than only some part or some area, as the special sciences do.

Whether this holistic knowledge is a valid aim, whether it is possible to be such a generalist, whether there are universals that are knowable, is the question that divides Platonists and anti-Platonists throughout the history of philosophy. It divides two kinds of colleges and universities in America today. Some see philosophy merely as a post script and a service department. Others, the minority today, see it as substantive and central.

Are we satisfied with partial, particular knowledge, or are we dissatisfied until we find wholes, universal Forms? To aim at the universal is also to be dissatisfied, to be more idealistic, more demanding.

This dissatisfaction means personal involvement, personal passion. Philosophy betrays itself when it turns into an impersonal academic "subject." Philosophy is not a "subject" for Plato; it is a love, an *eros*, a hunger. To be a philosopher, according to Plato, we have to be hungry. We have to be invested in the drama of ideas to understand them; we can never sit back passively and be amused by them like spectators at a movie. To use the food analogy, the dialogs are culinary adventures in cooking, not precooked TV dinners. So they are really impossible to summarize, for their logical summary is only one dimension of them. The psychological dimension is even more important, for that's what the logic is there for, for the personal drama of conversion, the healing of souls. Socrates, like Jesus and Buddha, is never simply a professor, a lecturer or writer, as are almost all other philosophers beginning with Aristotle.

The only other philosophers I can think of who give us this personal dimension as well as the logical—who aim at converting, turning us around one hundred eighty degrees, changing our very selves, not just our thoughts—are Augustine, Pascal, and

Kierkegaard—and Nietzsche, as the polar opposite of all three. For Nietzsche, the cave is precisely Plato's world of Forms and their metaphysical home in the Judeo-Christian God. More later on Nietzsche as the total anti-Platonist.

So we can imagine each Socratic dialog as a hunting expedition and the Form that the dialog seeks as the animal that's being hunted.

Thus the *Symposium* hunts for the Form of Love. That's why it's probably Plato's most popular and beautifully written dialog.

The *Republic* is, of course, about justice, the same Form in both the individual soul and in the city-state. Book 1 of the *Republic* is a typical early Socratic dialog, in which Socrates, after logically refuting three wrong definitions of justice, is left with no right one and is dissatisfied because he hasn't yet found the Form. And the practical payoff, the reason we need to find it, is because without it we can't prove that justice is more profitable than injustice, that it alone brings *happiness*. That's why the *Republic* is so important: it's about the most important question in the world, the good for man, the greatest good, the meaning of life, how to live. By the end of book 1, Socrates has proved this conclusion by logical argument—that justice is always profitable—but we are not convinced, and he does not expect us to be convinced, because we did not know what we were talking about, we did not know the Form, the essence, the real nature, of Justice. It takes three hundred more pages to do that.

Book 1 only climbed as high as the third step of the Divided Line (logical reasoning) but not the fourth and highest step (the understanding of the essence). Once we get that, three hundred pages later, through Plato's long political detour which shows us the hard-to-find invisible Form of justice in the soul by first showing us the easier-to-find, visible public Form of justice in the state—once we know the Form of justice, we are then and only then totally convinced that it is for our profit, our good, our happiness. We *see* it, not just calculate it; we understand it. That is the goal of every dialog: the understanding of *what* it is, and that is the only thing that totally convinces us and satisfies us. That's the fourth and highest step in our education.

The *Republic* argues that philosophy is needed for societies as well as for souls, because only the knowledge of the Forms can judge the shadows on the Divided Line and in the cave; only the knowledge of ideal justice can understand and repair real injustices. As Socrates argues, "If a shuttle is broken in the making, will the maker make a second one looking to the broken one as his standard, or will he look to the Form according to which he made the first one?"

What is true of shuttles is also true of states, and of souls, that is, of persons. Only if we know the design for a person do we know what it is to *be* one, and how to judge success in being one, how to avoid getting A's in your subjects but flunking Life.

The early dialogs always seek to know and define the Form of a particular virtue: friendship in the *Lysis*, courage in the *Laches*, temperance in the *Charmides*.

The *Philebus* is about the essential nature of pleasure and its relation to the supreme Good.

The *Phaedrus* explores the nature of mystical experience, divine madness, which is what happens when we find the Form of Beauty.

The *Phaedo* hunts for the meaning of death. Plato first argues about it and then actually presents it, at the end, with the most moving scene in all the world's literature outside the Gospels, the death of Socrates. When the idea of death and the idea of Socrates thus meet in our minds, it is the idea of death that is changed.

The *Meno* seems to hunt for the nature of virtue, which it never finds, but it really hunts for the nature of education, of teaching and learning, which it does find as a remembering of the Forms which we all already know unconsciously, so that philosophical education is like intellectual psychoanalysis, bringing our unconscious wisdom to the light of consciousness.

The *Theaetetus* hunts for the Form of knowledge, which is distinguished from both bodily sense perception and mere opinion or belief.

The *Gorgias* is the one dialog I'd have everyone read if I had to choose only one, because it's like the *Republic* without the politics. It's about the Good, the greatest good, the *summum bonum*, the meaning of life.

The *Parmenides* is about unity, or "the One"—a Form as elusive and as absolute as the Good and the Beautiful, for these three are ultimately three names for the same reality. All other forms are plural, and fit on the fourth and highest step of the *Republic's* Divided Line; but the One, or the Good, is above them all because all the other forms participate in it. It is the one absolutely absolute absolute, and it is single, and it is infinite. And that was a rare admission for a Greek to make, for infinity, to the typical ancient Greek mind, was an imperfection, not a perfection. To the Greek mind, only matter was infinite, and formless, and therefore imperfect; only finite form made it perfect, as it does in any work of art.

But in the *Republic* Socrates amazed his hearers by saying that the Good is infinite, and therefore not definable like other forms, like justice, but it can only be known through analogy, parable, symbol. It's like the sun. The sun gives light, and light symbolizes truth, definable truth; but the Good itself transcends definition as the sun transcends its light, as its source. The sun is not a lit object. You can't shine a light on the sun. It is the source of all light as the Idea of the Good is the source of all truth. Everything is what it is because it is somehow good. The good, the end, the point, and purpose—what Aristotle would call the final cause—is the ultimate explanation and truth of anything.

This Good is also Beauty. Beauty is not definable as a Form in the *Symposium* either, but only reached by a kind of mystical experience after ascending all the rungs of a spiritual ladder.

Not surprisingly, the *Sophist* is about the Sophist, and the *Statesman* is about the statesman, and the *Laws* is about the laws.

The *Ion* is about the arts, especially the art of rhetoric, and how it differs from philosophical wisdom, because it does not know the abstract universal, only the concrete particular. The dialog also shows how the power of great art is a matter of divine inspiration.

The *Cratylus* is about the essence of language, and about the myth of an original, archetypal language, which was the Platonic form and ideal for all later languages. (Plato takes this myth seriously, and that seems reasonable to me. They must have spoken *some* language in the Garden of Eden, after all, and I don't think it was Esperanto.)

The *Critias* is about the form or pattern of history, and finds its essential nature to be cyclical and devolutionary—a most unmodern view.

The *Timaeus* is about the essential nature of the physical universe, and the four causes of its creation. Aristotle's four causes, perhaps the most universally useful organizing principle in the history of human thought, depend directly on the four eternals in Plato's *Timaeus*: (1) the Forms; (2) the receptacle of form, which is matter or space; (3) the agent or maker of the universe who imposes form on matter; and (4) the Good as the motive and end of all creation. Aristotle called these the formal, material, efficient, and final causes.

Finally, there is no dialog about the most important thing of all, Plato's big idea, the Idea of the Good itself. In his *Seventh Letter*, he refers to a book that was circulating in Athens entitled *On the Good* by Plato, and he says it's a fake. He would never write such a book, he says, because the Good, the ultimate Good, which is Plato's equivalent of God, can be known only when two minds strike each other together in the search for truth like flint and steel and produce a sudden spark, like lightning.

That's what has to happen when you read Plato: a lightning bolt suddenly hits your mind if you are in dialog with Plato and with yourself, if you identify with all the characters—if this dialog happens in your soul as well as in your book, you have an "aha!" experience. You *see*. And then you know a tiny bit of heaven, for just a split second. If in that second you could *just see* the What of *everything*—why, then you would know why God never gets bored. And then perhaps you would look forward to dying with hope and excitement, as a baby looks forward to being born, and as a prisoner looks forward to escaping from his cave.

Plato wrote his dialogs to help us to do exactly that. That's the meaning of education, real education, which means literally "a leading out." I know no better way to begin your education than reading Plato's dialogs, and I wish you all an exciting journey and a happy ending.

Lecture III:
Three Additions to Plato:
Aristotle, Plotinus, and Augustine

Modern philosophy consists mainly of subtractions from Plato. There are subtractions from Plato in ancient philosophy too, especially ancient skepticism and the materialism of both the Stoics and the Epicureans. But Aristotle and Plotinus and Augustine added rather than subtracted from the Platonic tradition, as Plato added to Socrates.

Aristotle added essentially the presence of the Forms in the material world. He was a Platonist in that he did not deny the Forms, only their separation from material things. He did not deny them but brought them closer, as a Christian does not deny the transcendent God of Jews and Muslims but brings Him closer by the Incarnation.

Plotinus added essentially two kinds of mysticism, objective and subjective: objectively, in speaking of the unspeakable, the Form of the Absolute One, and subjectively, in his detailed description of the mystical ascent to this One.

Augustine added the metaphysical address of the Forms: the Mind of God. They are Ideas, and ideas without a mind seems impossible. They are, of course, in our minds when we think of them, but since we are temporal, they cannot always be there. The Ideas are eternal and therefore there must be an eternal Mind for them to eternally reside in. Thus Augustine uses Plato's Ideas, and our knowledge of them, to prove the existence of God.

Let's look more carefully at each of these three great additions to the Platonic tradition.

Aristotle is the one that's not usually called an addition, but a subtraction, or at least a radical alternative. It's *not* a radical alternative. Aristotle is a Platonist. If you want a first-rate philosopher and historian to prove that, read A. E. Taylor's little book, *Aristotle.*

Aristotle does not deny the existence of the Forms. They are as central to his philosophy as they are to Plato's. He is always on the hunt for a Form, a universal, a real essence. Modern philosophers shun Aristotle because of this, because of his Platonism. What Aristotle denies is the *chorismos,* the separation, of the Forms, in three areas: metaphysics, epistemology, and anthropology.

In his metaphysics, he denies that the Forms exist in a separate, spiritual world of their own. They exist only in this world. And that "only" is indeed a subtraction (of the second, separate "world") from Plato. And perhaps it's not that much of an addition either, for Plato too said that things "participate" in the Forms. In that sense his Forms are not only transcendent, they are also immanent—rather like God.

In his epistemology, Aristotle denies Plato's doctrine of *anamnesis,* or recollection: that we have innate ideas of the Forms and need only to remember them under the prod of Socratic questioning. Since they exist in matter, we have to go out and abstract them from matter, like a hunter abstracting a lion from the jungle. So all our learning begins with sense perception. That is really an addition, as the jungle is an addition to the zoo.

Finally, in Aristotle's anthropology, just as a Form makes up one substance with its matter, so man is not merely his Form (which is his rational human soul), but rather the substance made of both matter and form, body and soul. Aristotle agrees that what makes us distinctively human is our rational soul, so he essentially agrees with Plato, but he adds the body too as part of our essence. He defined man as a rational *animal.*

The practical consequences of this are clear in his *Ethics.* It begins by seeking the good for man, which is happiness, as Plato says, and it defines this as an active life according to virtue, as Plato also says. While Aristotle adds eight other virtues to Plato's four cardinal virtues (justice, wisdom, courage, and moderation), he also begins with and concentrates on these four. But then he adds "in a complete life" and "with sufficient bodily goods" to Plato's definition of happiness. This addition is only secondary; and like Plato, Aristotle says that even with a minimum of bodily goods and in the presence of ordinary suffering, happiness is attainable, for the good and wise man makes the most of whatever fate brings him. But bodily goods count a little bit, at least. So Aristotle is 90 percent Plato but with a 10 percent addition, a reminder that our bodies are us too, not just motel rooms, not just places where we visit, as houses are haunted by ghosts. (But of course Plato did not think of the soul as a ghost any more than Aristotle did.)

To see how Platonic Aristotle is, look at his epistemology. He divides knowledge into four kinds. The lowest kind is unscientific knowledge, and the three kinds of scientific knowledge are three degrees of abstraction, three degrees of universality (for like Plato, Aristotle defines scientific knowledge as knowledge of universals, which means knowledge of Forms). There are three levels of scientific knowledge for Aristotle: (1) physics, which understands universal physical laws (physical Forms) by abstracting from individual physical matter; and then (2) mathematics, which also abstracts from change and uncovers truths that are changeless, whereas physics deals with the world of time and change and motion; and finally (3) metaphysics, which abstracts from all particularity. This is really Plato's Divided Line! Nonscientific knowledge is the lowest quarter; *eikasia* is his word for it: the imaginary, the knowledge of shadows. The second level is the perception of material things, which Plato called *pistis* (belief), because it trusts the senses. The third level, *dianoia*, is logic and mathematics, which uses step by step reasoning from a hypothesis or premise. Finally the fourth level is *episteme*, certain knowledge, the intellectual intuition of an unchangeable Form, without matter. Both Plato and Aristotle make the highest kind of knowledge this direct intellectual intuition of a Form.

For both thinkers, *episteme* is reached by starting at the bottom of the line and climbing step by step. So Plato too begins with imagination and sense perception and even mere opinion (*doxa*)—

the opinions of Socrates's dialog partner. He does not omit these lower parts of knowledge but uses them as rungs on his ladder to climb above them, which is what Aristotle does too. The only important difference is Aristotle's theory of abstraction of form from matter rather than recollection of innate ideas of the Forms. In both cases, we use logical deduction—level three of the line— to ascend to level four, which is certainty.

Both believe we can attain certainty. And this, I think, is what sets them most deeply at odds with the typically modern mind. If there is one thing that will not be tolerated by moderns it is the claim to certainty. Test that claim at a fashionable cocktail party some time. Confess to believing any number of strange ideas and no one will dispute with you but confess to certainty about any-thing important, such as moral absolutes, or immortality, or, worst of all, God, and you will be looked at as if you never used soap.

Both Plato and Aristotle believe reality culminates in a single perfect God, who is eternal Form without matter. Both believe the universe is ordered hierarchically into kinds, species, immutably different Forms. Both believe in teleology, final causality, objective purpose, for everything, or as it's called today, "intelligent de-sign." Those two words are as unacceptable today among the chattering classes as the two words "Great Books." "Unintelligent randomness" is much more popular than intelligent design, just as Great Books have been replaced by "dumbed-down little books" for dumbed-down little minds.

Both Plato and Aristotle believe in two dimensions of reality, matter and form. Both distinguish soul and body, intellect and senses, rational moral will and animal desires. Both believe that the end of life is happiness, which comes only with the intellec-tual and moral virtues. Both believe in education, and that the end of all education, including political education, is for you to be formed by timeless truth and thus realize your human nature, your essence, your Form. For modern education, the end is free-dom or self-realization, something subjective, and then trans-forming objective reality, which is thought of as only the material world, to conform to your desires, rather than transforming your desires to conform to the objective reality of the spiritual world.

For both Plato and Aristotle, in fact for all premodern thinkers except the skeptics and the Sophists, truth is objective and we can know it. They are all epistemological realists: we can know reality, our mind can discover and conform to objective reality. Reason is open to reality and reality is open to reason. This is not so for Hume or Kant or Nietzsche, who are probably the three most influential modern philosophers, as we shall see in a later lecture.

Both Plato and Aristotle find *hierarchy* to be so essential everywhere that they assume it rather than proving it. Today, this is the very last thing modernists can admit. Plato and Aristotle place form over matter, eternity over time, gods over men, men over animals, virtue over vice, soul over body, reason over passions, and the political order of wise and just rulers over citizens (though Aristotle defends representative democracy as one of these just orders, and Plato does not).

Above all, both Plato and Aristotle tell us to live according to reason, because reason is not just subjective cleverness but the understanding of the nature of things.

Now there's a lot more in Aristotle that's not in Plato, and some of it is indeed an alternative to Plato, and contradicts Plato. But it's mostly details. I've given you the Big Picture, which is often forgotten by philosophy books and teachers, as you often forget the names of the countries when you look at the towns on a map. Plato and Aristotle live in adjoining towns in the same country; we live in a different country, a brave new world, in which an idea is only an opinion, a form is only a shape, an end is only a personal motive, a substance is only a chemical, happiness is only a feeling, virtue is only prudery, justice is only legality, souls are only religious superstitions, and judgments that claim objective truth are only judgmentalism and intolerance.

Even Aristotle's overt disagreements with Plato turn into agreements in the end. He begins by emphasizing nature as self-explaining, without the transcendent Ideas, but he ends by making nature dependent on God, who is even more transcendent than Platonic Ideas because nature does not participate in God.

He begins by opposing Empiricism and abstraction to Plato's rationalism and innate ideas, but he ends by founding all knowledge on self-evident first principles like the law of non-contradiction, which are innately known, not abstracted.

He begins by making the primary object of knowledge the sensible substance rather than the immaterial Form, but he ends by saying that the ultimate knowledge is the knowledge of God, who is immaterial substance

He begins by giving the material world something real of its own, not just a reflection of the Forms. But he ends by saying matter is not actual, only potential. All the actuality in any substance is due to the form, not the matter.

He begins by making the soul the form of the body. But he ends by making the agent intellect, the active intellect, even more independent and divine than Plato's soul.

He begins by criticizing Plato's Socratic thesis that evil is ignorance and the good is knowledge, but he ends by identifying the supreme good, in the *Ethics*, with intellectual contemplation of eternal truths.

In general, he criticizes Plato for being too otherworldly, and all the history of philosophy books present him as more this-worldly, realistic, and pragmatic than Plato. Yet he says that the ultimate end of philosophy is wisdom and wisdom is the knowledge of God. which means two things: our knowledge of God and the knowledge that God alone has, so that only God is truly wise, just as Socrates said. And the highest form of our knowledge of God is contemplation, not proof.

In sum, four phrases summarize the difference between Aristotle and Plato: (1) hylomorphism in metaphysics; (2) empiricism and abstraction in epistemology; (3) the psychosomatic unity in anthropology; and (4) this-worldly happiness in ethics. All four are only secondary corrections, and Aristotle's essential

Platonism shows through in all four, for form is still more important than matter, intellect than senses, soul than body, and divine contemplation than the satisfaction of this-worldly desires.

Aristotle was Plato's prime pupil for 20 years in his Academy. He waited until Plato died to set up his own school, the Lyceum, and did so with the famous apology, "dear, indeed, is Plato, but dearer still is truth." In the end, it turns out the two were not very radically different.

Plotinus founded Neoplatonism, over five hundred years after Aristotle's death in 322 BC, and he influenced the Middle Ages more than Plato or Aristotle did, since they knew him better. Plato's works were not rediscovered until the early years of the Renaissance, and Aristotle's not until the thirteenth century.

Unlike Aristotle, Plotinus always considered himself a totally faithful disciple of Plato rather than an alternative. Yet in some ways Plotinus's addition was more radical than Aristotle's, and more of a subtraction.

For one thing, Plotinus denied the rationality, the intelligibility, of ultimate reality, of Plato's Idea of the Good. He sharply separated this ultimate reality, which he called "The One," from the realm of the Ideas.

For another thing, Plotinus said matter was the source of evil, and he had a deep hatred and fear of matter and the body.

Finally, Plotinus could never have written a *Republic* or a *Laws*, for interpersonal justice, harmony, and community, which were very high on Plato's list of values, were definitely low on Plotinus's list. Here is his most famous passage, describing the ultimate end of human life, attainable only by the mystic:

> "This is the life of the gods and of the divine and the happy among men: a liberation from all this-worldly concerns, a life unaccompanied by human pleasures, a flight of the alone to the Alone."

Obviously these features of Neoplatonism are both compatible and incompatible with Christianity. They are compatible insofar as they emphasize the transcendence of God over human concepts, of the soul over the body, of heaven over earth, and of the individual's ultimate destiny in the Beatific Vision over earthly politics and community; but incompatible insofar as they denigrate human reason, matter, the body, this world, and community. Plotinus knew of Christianity and vehemently rejected it because of these Incarnational emphases. Yet the Christian Middle Ages were deeply influenced by Neoplatonism, and most of the heresies in the early Church were inspired by Gnosticism, which was an offshoot of Neoplatonism. Yet great orthodox Christian theologians like Augustine knew and admired and used much of Neoplatonism, because of the compatibilities—for instance, the Neoplatonists helped Augustine overcome his materialistic, imaginative, spatial images of God. Aquinas summarizes Augustine's Neoplatonism very simply and accurately this way: "When Augustine, who was imbued with the doctrines of the Platonists, found anything compatible with the Faith, he adopted it, and when he found anything incompatible, he rejected it."

I think the main fascination with Plotinus was that he expanded the experiential, mystical dimension to Plato, especially the famous Ladder of Love in the *Symposium*. The only one of the 81 treatises of Plotinus that was preserved for the Middle Ages was the first one, the treatise on Beauty, yet this gave a fair and profound sample of the heart of his philosophy.

For instance, take the following passage. Beauty is "something detected at first glance, something that the soul, remembering, names, recognizes, gives welcome to, and in a way fuses with. When the soul falls in with ugliness, it shrinks back, repulses it, turns away from it as alien. We suggest that the reason for this experience is that the soul, being what it is and related to the reality above it, is delighted when it sees any signs of kinship, anything akin to itself, takes its own into itself, and is stirred to new awareness of whence and what it really is...What is this kinship? What can they have in common, beauty here and beauty

42

there? They have, we suggest, this in common: they are sharers of the same Idea."

Look how Plotinus interprets our fascination with fire by this Platonic metaphysics: "That is why fire glows with a beauty beyond all other bodies, for fire holds the rank of Idea in relation to them. Always struggling aloft, this subtlest of all elements is at the last limits of the bodily. It admits no other into itself, while all other bodies give it entry." This also explains our fascination with music: "in the realm of sound, unheard harmonies create the harmonies we hear."

And when we come to perceive the Platonic Idea of Beauty itself with the soul, Plotinus says, "we undergo a joy, a wonder, and a distress more deep than any other because here one touches truth. For beauty is genuine reality; ugliness, its opposite. . . . Such emotion all beauty must induce: an astonishment, a delicious wonderment, a longing, a love, a trembling that is all delight. . . . All perceive it. Not all are stung sharply by it. Only they whom we call lovers ever are."

Plotinus describes mystical experience by comparing it to a person so absorbed in reading that he is unaware that he is reading, or even that he exists. He is no longer conscious of himself as the subject; he is now wholly identified with the object. This is what happens whenever we have "peak experiences": a blissful loss of self-consciousness. Most Hindus and Buddhists interpret this experience as an "enlightenment" or waking up from the illusion or dream that we *are* individual subjects of consciousness. But both Plotinus and Plato, and most Western mystics, interpret it not as a denial of the reality of the individual soul but as the soul's attainment of its ultimate destiny and perfection in stepping out of its own shadow of self-consciousness. Self-consciousness always ruins the bliss of these peak experiences. Once you start thinking, "I am now having a mystical experience," you're instantly *out* of the experience.

This mysticism is suggested in Plato's *Symposium* and *Phaedrus*. But Plotinus added two things to Plato: much more detail of the experience itself, and another level of metaphysics above Plato's, a kind of impersonal Trinity of principles that he said explained the world we see. Lowest of the three, and between Plato's Ideas and the world, was the "world soul," the efficient cause of all life and motion and time (but not the cause of matter, as the biblical God is the creator of matter). This "world-soul" corresponds roughly to Plato's creator-god or Demiurge in the *Timaeus*, and to Aristotle's efficient cause. Above this was the super-cosmic Intelligence, in which resided all the Platonic Ideas, a kind of impersonal divine mind. This corresponds to Aristotle's formal cause. Above even this was the One, which he identified with Plato's Idea of the Good, so this corresponds to Aristotle's final cause, at least in how it functions as the end of everything else.

(The fourth Aristotelian cause, the material cause, is no part of this Plotinian trinity, but is the source of darkness and ugliness and evil.)

The One as the Good functions as final cause but it is not immanent in things, as it is for Aristotle, and it is not a God, a Person, as it is for Christianity, and it is not a Platonic Form, because it is not intelligible, not definable. It is beyond Intelligence, and even, Plotinus said, "beyond being." Now this is a very strange thing to say. "Beyond being" sounds like "unreal" or 'nonexistent." But Plotinus means almost the opposite, something like "more real than being." What could that possibly mean?

Plotinus meant by "being" not "existence" but "intelligible essence" or "intelligibility." So the transcendent One *is*, but it has no *essence*. But everything knowable has a knowable, intelligible essence. Therefore the One is unknowable.

Or instead of saying that the One is unknowable because it's beyond being, you could say that it's beyond being because it's unknowable. For it's absolutely one, not dual, while all knowledge implies a duality of knower and known, subject and object.

Another argument for the One's unknowability is from its infinity. Both intelligence and its objects are finite, but the One is infinite, and therefore it is not an object of intelligence or a subject of intelligence. It neither knows nor is known. Instead of being an *object* of intelligence, it is the transcendent source and origin of intelligence. It's like Brahman in the Hindu scriptures, the *Upanishads*, "the one without a Second." This, by the way, clearly distinguishes it from both the Jewish God, who by creating the world becomes the one *with* a second, and the Christian God, who even in Himself is one *with* a second and a third divine Person in the Trinity.

Plotinus's Trinity of One, Intelligence, and World-Soul is very different from the Christian Trinity, by the way, for two reasons: first, it is not three *persons* and second, because the three are unequal. They are not one being. Since Plotinus meant by "being" simply "essence," not existence, and since essences are many, he concluded that the One, being beyond many-ness and therefore beyond essence, was beyond being. The One is "beyond being" as Plotinus is beyond Plato.

Augustine was a Christian Platonist. It's often said that he "baptized Platonism." Augustine's Christianity was not for him a postscript to Plato; Plato was a prescript to Christianity. Augustine was not a Platonist who happened to be a Christian but a Christian who happened to be a Platonist.

No other philosophers ever excelled Plato and Augustine in uniting the two essential qualities of rational philosophy and of human personality, head and heart, intellect and imagination, rationalism and romanticism, logic and poetry, objectivity and subjectivity, clarity and profundity, the theoretical and the practical, the impersonal and the personal, critical questioning and humble personal piety. Medieval statuary of Augustine always has him holding an open book in one hand and a burning heart in the other.

His philosophy is Platonic in many ways. He agrees with Plato that the true self is the soul (though he thinks the body is much more important than Plato did, as Plato thought it was more important than Plotinus did).

He agrees with Plato that true knowledge comes from the soul and its intellect, not the body and its senses, which yield only opinions and uncertainty. He uses Plato's interior road to truth rather than Aristotle's exterior, empirical road. In fact, this interior road is his argument for God: our temporal minds can know eternal truth, therefore there must be an eternal mind in which we see this truth. He writes: "Do not go abroad. Return within yourself. Truth dwells in the inward man." And when we find truth there, the *there* is adverbial, not adjectival: it modifies the finding, not the truth. The truth is objective, above the mind. He argues; when I mentally see some eternal, certain truth, like $2 + 2 = 4$, and you see it too, where is it? I see it *with* my mind but not *in* my mind. It is objective to my mind, as rocks are objective to my body. Where is it, then? Not in your mind. When we both see that $2 + 2 = 4$, I do not see it in your mind and you do not see it in my mind; but we both see it in the something that exists above both our minds and which judges both our minds. This can only be the Mind of God, which is the house in which Plato's Ideas live. This he identified with the pre-incarnate Christ, the divine *Logos*.

Augustine reconciled the plurality of the Platonic Ideas with the singleness of the Mind of God by using the human analogy that we too have a single mind but many ideas.

Augustine is also Platonic in agreeing that knowing the Ideas is done not by sense perception or abstraction but by a divine illumination from above. But for Augustine this is not a remembering from previous reincarnations or from a previous life in Heaven, as Plato suggested. But for both Plato and Augustine, and for Plotinus too, knowledge of the eternal truth happens during a kind of "aha!" experience.

Most history of philosophy textbooks will tell you that Augustine's essential contribution to Platonism was to fill in an intellectual lacuna or hole in Plato's metaphysics, to answer the question Plato left unanswered about the Platonic Ideas, namely, where are they? They are not anywhere in space, of course, but how can any Ideas just *be* without a mind in which they are? They are not merely human ideas, not merely ideas *in* our minds. They

are divine ideas, and so they need a divine mind. That was Augustine's contribution: he gave a home to the homeless Ideas. There was a perfect fit between Augustine's Christian God and Plato's Ideas, like the fit between the Queen of England and Buckingham Palace. Especially because the Christian God is supremely intelligent, and because His intelligence, His Mind, His *Logos*, His Word, is what St. John the Evangelist identified Jesus with: the divine *Logos* became human flesh in the Incarnation.

This is all true, but I think this standard line misses the deepest point. I think the essential contribution of Augustine to Platonism is not merely the solution to an intellectual problem in metaphysics. For Augustine the *Logos* is not a concept. A concept is weaker than what it knows. My concept of human nature is weaker than human nature itself; the concept is less than the reality. But the *Logos* is more. It is the Mind of the Maker and Modeler. It is the Model and Standard and Archetype.

Augustine didn't merely join Plato's forms with the Christian God: he expanded Plato's Forms by expanding Plato's God. For Augustine God is a Person, and a Person has a will or a heart as well as a mind; and the essential function of the will or the heart, according to Augustine, is to love. As the physical heart is the center of the physical body, the spiritual heart, the power to love, is the center of the soul. And this new centering on love expands Plato's concept of man as well as Plato's concept of God.

How? Here is Augustine's essential anthropology. For Augustine, there are two fundamentally different kinds of people in the world, and these two kinds of people make up the "two cities," the City of God and the City of the World. All the people who have ever lived who have chosen God as the ultimate object of their love, however clearly or obscurely they have known God, are members of the City of God, and destined for eternal union with God in Heaven, since everyone eventually gets what they want, what they love. "*Amor meus pondus meum* (my love is my weight, my gravity, my destiny)," Augustine says. And everyone whose ultimate love is this world and themselves, not God, will

eternally get that, and not God, and they will be eternally unhappy because all human hearts are designed to be happy only by getting what they are designed to love, namely God.

In other words, Augustine essentially adds three h's to Plato: larger views of hearts, heaven, and hell.

Augustine is a perfect example of the Hamlet principle: "There are more things in heaven and earth, Horatio, / Than are dreamt of in your philosophy." The real thing is bigger than the biggest concept. Augustine saw clearly, as Plato did not, that persons are greater than ideas—in fact, that divinity is person, not idea.

That's why Jesus in the New Testament isn't boring, as Jesus in most sermons is. That's why Jesus never bored anybody in the world, though most books about him do. And that's why Augustine says—in the rightly famous sentence that's the key to his *Confessions*, and to all our lives—that our hearts are restless until they rest in God because He has made us for Himself. And that's why our hearts are bigger than the universe, since they are able to know and to love, as the universe is not, and therefore our hearts need something even bigger than themselves to fulfill them, not something smaller than themselves, like everything in the universe. One of the things smaller than ourselves is a concept. *Logos* is not a concept for Augustine. *Logos* is God, the Mind of God, the Word of God. And Jesus is the *Logos* become flesh. The house where all Plato's Ideas live was an eternal Person who became a temporal person: the Mind of the Author put Himself into the story He designed as one of his own characters. For Augustine, Jesus is both transcendent and immanent—like Plato's Ideas, and yet very unlike them.

So Augustine is a Christian Platonist. But it was Plotinus and Socrates rather than Plato himself that influenced Augustine the most.

Let's look at these two connections. First, Augustine read Plotinus, and probably never read Plato himself. In his *Confessions* he speaks of "some books of the Platonists" and credits them with

freeing him from many errors about God by freeing him from materialistic thinking. But he also faults the Platonists for showing him the goal without the way to it, the end without the means, the soul's heaven without the earthly path to it.

The other connection is with Socrates. Of course he never read Socrates, because Socrates never wrote anything. And if he never read the dialogs of Plato, he never confronted the historical Socrates, not even secondhand through Plato, but only third hand, through Platonists. Yet Augustine is closer to the spirit of Socrates than any other philosopher has ever been, I think. He thinks Socratically, dialectically, dialogically; he's always dialoging with himself and with God. The *Confessions* has a larger percentage of interrogative sentences in it than any other philosophical classic except actual dialogs. And with regard to actual dialogs, no one has ever come closer to writing a genuine Socratic dialog than Augustine did, in *On the Teacher*, which he tells us was an actual dialog with his 16-year-old son, Adeodatus, who died shortly after. It's brilliant, and so is Adeodatus, who might have become a second Augustine if he had lived. Strange and wonderful are the ways of Divine Providence. In fact, that's the main theme of the *Confessions*.

Lecture IV:
Christian Platonism

The main way Platonism influenced Western civilization is through Christianity. In this lecture I want to sample six Christian Platonists, three writers in the New Testament (Jesus, John, and Paul) and three philosophers (Justin Martyr, Bonaventure, and Aquinas).

All six presuppose and use, as their background and foundation, the most Platonic verse in the Old Testament, Genesis 2:7, which says that God created man "in His own image." The notion of image is the fundamental metaphysical relationship in Plato's philosophy, the relationship that connects the three kinds of reality. As *our* ideas are images of the things in the world, the things in the world are images of *the* Ideas. All concrete material beings on earth, including man, are images of the eternal archetypes, which Augustine located in the Mind of God.

We can't push this connection with Plato too far. There are at least three important differences between Plato and the Bible.

First, the Bible does not teach a Platonic realm of eternal, abstract, universal essences, because the Bible is not a book of abstract philosophy. What is eternal in the Bible is a single concrete, immaterial being who is a person (though not a human person), whose name is I AM, who is a subject, not just an object, as Plato's Ideas are.

Second, in the Bible man alone is made in God's image because man alone is a person, a subject, a knower and lover. The concept of image is not used for nature, although nature is designed by God and *implicitly* images the ideas in His mind, His wisdom.

Third, in the Bible the image of God in man is centered in the heart, or the will, the faculty of loving and choosing, more than

50

in the mind—though the distinction between the two is not sharp, and the same word, "heart," in the Bible sometimes means mind and sometimes will and sometimes feelings and sometimes something more primordial and mysterious than either mind, or will, or feelings.

Yet the notion God's image in man is a connector between the two worlds in the Bible as well as in Plato.

Our first Christian thinker is Christ himself. If Christ was not a Christian, nobody ever was. And he certainly was a thinker! Now according to Christianity, Christ was not merely a 33-year-long, six-feet-high Jewish carpenter, but also the eternal Son of God, the Mind of God, the Designer of man and the universe, and therefore the Mind that *designed* Plato. So when we find Christ saying something Platonic, that's no coincidence.

And we do find Him Platonizing. It was one of the ways He startled his hearers. (He *always* startled his hearers, by the way.)

Where does Jesus Platonize? In John 4, where he explains to his disciples, when they forget to bring food in the wilderness, "My food is to do the will of My Father." That's soul food, but that's real food, and physical food is an image of that. He turns our minds upside down. What we think is the real thing, He takes as an image; and what we think is an image He says is the real thing. That's Platonism. Matter images spirit.

Let's look next at how Paul uses this same Platonic reversal. In Ephesians 3:14 he writes, "I bow my knees before the Father from whom every family in heaven and on earth is named." We think of "God the Father" as a metaphor or image, but Paul reverses this and says that our earthly fathers and families are metaphors or images of what fatherhood and family really is, namely God's Fatherhood over Christ His Son and the Trinity as the Ultimate Family after whom all earthly families are named because they are created in God's image.

Jesus Himself called God his Father, and told us to call God our Father too, in giving us the Lord's Prayer. It's the same reversed metaphor. Earthly fatherhood is the metaphor, the image of the one perfect Platonic archetypal Fatherhood of God, in eternity over His Son and in time over us.

Paul also uses the Platonic notion of image for Jesus Himself, in Colossians, when he writes, "He is the image of the invisible God. . . . For in him all the fullness of God was pleased to dwell" (Col 1:15, 1:19).

The classic passage in the New Testament for Christian Platonism is John 1, where John identifies Christ with the *Logos*. That Greek word has literally dozens of meanings, but one of them is something like The Ultimate Truth about the Nature of All Things, or The Mind of God. John first says "In the beginning was the *Logos*, and the *Logos* was with God and the *Logos* was God." (*Logos* means Reason or Mind or Inner Word or Thought; and your thoughts are both *with* you *and* they *are* you; the thinker and his thought are both one and two.) And then John makes the astonishing statement that "the *Logos* became flesh and dwelt among us." Eternal Truth got born from Mary's womb; the heavenly house where all of Plato's Ideas live became a human being.

This equation of Jesus and the *Logos* is a double expansion, a double moreness. It claims that Jesus is more than he seems to be, more than a human being; He is the *Logos*. And it also says that the *Logos* is more than it seems to be: it is not just an abstract impersonal truth, but a divine person who became also human.

Greek philosophers had always sought the *Logos*, as Odysseus sought his home or Jason sought the Golden Fleece. The word has literally dozens of related meanings, but they can be brought under three headings: metaphysical, psychological, and linguistic. *Logos* means, first of all, realness, authenticity, truth, intelligibility, meaning, essence, form, order, structure, point, purpose, relationship, unity, principle, or universal. It also meant, in the second place, wisdom, understanding, knowledge, sagacity, intelligence, thought, explanation, reason, or logic: the human, psychological internalization of the first *Logos*, the metaphysical

Logos. Finally, it also means word, words, language, speech, communication, revelation, expression, manifestation, argument, discourse, testimony, witness, or explanation. *Logos* #3 is a mind's externalization of *Logos* #2 as *Logos* #2 is a mind's internalization of *Logos* #1.

These are the three things Gorgias the Sophist denies. He summarize his philosophy in three sentences: First, There is no intelligible reality, no order and meaning to reality. Second, even if there were, it could never be known, never understood. Third, even if anyone did understand it, it could never be communicated. So Gorgias is the total alternative to Plato in his triple denial of *Logos*.

In fact, the whole history of philosophy has been structured by these three denials. Premodern philosophy, ancient and medieval, centered on metaphysics, and ended with the Nominalism of William of Ockham, which is a denial of *Logos* #1, intelligible universals. Then, classical Modern philosophy, beginning with Descartes and Bacon, centered on epistemology and ended in the empiricist skepticism of Hume and the even more radical skepticism of Kant, who denied that anyone could ever know things as they are in themselves, in other words objective reality. That's Gorgias's second thesis. Finally, twentieth-century philosophy concentrated on philosophy of language and culminated in Deconstructionism, which is the denial of *Logos* #3, the denial that words can tell truths.

All that—the whole subsequent history of philosophy—is at stake in *Logos*.

Logos means all three things: essence, thought, and language; or meaning, idea, and word; but it's translated "word" in John 1 because that includes all three meanings. If there is an expression, a word, as distinct from just noise, it must express knowledge; and if there is knowledge, not just feeling, it must know knowable, intelligible reality.

John is plugging Jesus into Genesis here, and the plug is Platonism. In the Genesis creation story, God creates the universe by His word, by first speaking words—and of course these are not physical words but mental words or Ideas—and then the things that these words mean come into existence. That is precisely Platonism: Plato's Ideas, unlike our ideas, are not copies of things but things are copies of them. God's Ideas are prior to things; ours are posterior to things. In us, words copy ideas and ideas copy things, but in God creating things the Ideas come first. And all these many Ideas are unified in the one Idea, or one Word, or one Divine Mind. That is the *Logos* which, John says, became incarnate in Jesus. So when John said that the *Logos* became flesh, he meant that what became the man Jesus was all three *Logoi*: the meaning of all things, and the wisdom that is the understanding of the meaning of all things, and the word that is the revelation of the wisdom that is the understanding of the meaning of all things. That's who Jesus is, according to Christianity. The claim is that Christ is the fulfillment of Platonism. And "if Plato is philosophy and philosophy is Plato," as Emerson said, then Christ is the fulfillment of philosophy.

For St. John, of course, not for Plato. We have no way of knowing what Plato would have said to this if he could have traveled forward in time some five hundred years and met the early Christians. Would he have thought them the wisest or the most insane thinkers who ever lived? Quite possibly the second. For they were saying something like "The meaning of life became a baby, and then a crucified criminal, and then a corpse, and then rose from the dead." This is the idea that Kierkegaard called "the absolute paradox": that eternity entered time, that the beginningless God acquired a beginning. Plato may well have called that impossible. For the Greeks, unlike the Jews, did not know any God of whom it could be truly said that "with God *all* things are possible."

But for the next five hundred years after John wrote, more and more philosophers did believe it, and for one thousand years after that *every* major philosopher in the West believed it.

What did they mean? How did they unite Christ and Plato, religion and philosophy, faith and reason?

We've already briefly covered the most historically influential one, Augustine. Let's look at three others: three of the most

Platonic and the most brilliant of Christian philosophers, Justin Martyr, Bonaventure, and Aquinas.

Already in the second century we find the typical pattern for the interaction between Platonic philosophy and Christianity in Justin's autobiographical account of his philosophical and religious journey. He was a pagan Roman who came to Athens to study philosophy. Philosophy in the ancient world was not just an academic or scholarly exercise but also a very personal and life-changing thing. In fact it was more like an alternative religion, a total way of life. After all, the word "philosophy" means "the love of wisdom," not "the game of cleverness." Justin says the aim of the philosophers had always been "to see God."

There were five main schools of philosophy in Justin's time: Platonism, Aristotelianism, Stoicism, Pythagoreanism, and Epicureanism, which was the only one that was atheistic and materialistic and subordinated wisdom to pleasure. Justin tried all four of the others. The Stoic philosopher he tried first disappointed Justin when he said that he neither knew God nor did he think this knowledge was necessary. Justin next went to an Aristotelian, who haggled so much over prepayment of tuition money that Justin thought "he was not a lover of wisdom but of money." Next he tried a Pythagorean, who refused to teach Justin philosophy because he had not studied mathematics. Finally he found a Platonist, and Justin wrote, "the contemplation of the Ideas gave my mind wings, so that after a little time I thought I had become wise, and I was even foolish enough to think that I was about to see God, for such is the aim of Plato's philosophy."

Then Justin met an old man on the beach, who discombobulated him by showing him some contradictions in Plato, especially about reincarnation: if after seeing God souls forget Him, and are reincarnated into earthly bodies, where is their eternal happiness? And how can reincarnation be a remedial punishment and an education if we don't remember what sins we committed in our previous reincarnation?

When Justin confessed that his whole purpose in studying philosophy was to see God, the old man disposed of all pagan philosophers with one question: "How should the philosophers judge truly about God when they do not know Him, since they have never seen Him or heard Him?" When Justin asked the man where he got his wisdom, he replied: Directly, from God's prophets, who did not need or use argumentation because they were actual first-hand witnesses of God, and proved it by miracles. And when the old man spoke of Christ, Justin said, "straightway a flame was kindled in my soul, and a love of the prophets and the friends of Christ possessed me, and I found this philosophy alone to be profitable. Thus, and for this reason I am a philosopher." Notice how he labeled his conversion: to Christianity and to true philosophy as the same thing. Justin then argued with the other pagan philosophers as the old man had done to him, and found that this new religion, though at first accepted by faith, was also the most rational philosophy.

Here, in a nutshell, is the experience not only of Justin but of nearly all classical Christian philosophers for the rest of time, and the basis of its dialog with Greek philosophy, especially Plato. There are three stages in the journey. First, Justin seeks wisdom by reason alone, and fails. Then, he accepts divinely revealed wisdom by faith. Finally, he finds that it alone satisfies his reason. He finds in the Christian religion the attainment of philosophical wisdom by non-philosophical methods.

Even though Justin is relatively simple and unsophisticated, he is the paradigm case for subsequent Christian philosophers. And "philosophy" meant "Platonism or Neoplatonism" to almost all of them for the first one thousand years of the Christian era. Justin sets the angle, so to speak. An inch of divergence between the two lines at the beginning of an angle can mean a mile's divergence farther from the point of origin. St. Augustine may have been the Plato of Christian philosophy and St. Thomas Aquinas its Aristotle, but Justin was its Socrates.

Even more important than Justin's *experience* for subsequent philosophers was his Platonic explanation and interpretation of the experience. Like Augustine a few centuries later, Justin found Plato an indispensable beginning, a sort of soil or fertilizer for the seed of faith. How did Plato know such wisdom? How could pagans know so much divine truth? Justin's answer was that they were in unconscious contact with the pre-incarnate Christ, the *Logos*, the ultimate source of all truth, the Mind of God.

And since Christ is the *Logos*—this expands the notion of Christ—the *Logos* is also Christ—and this expands the notion of the *Logos*. John said of Christ that He is "the light that enlightens every man who comes into the world." This means, then, that, to use Justin's own words,

> "Since He is the *Logos* of whom every race of men are partakers, therefore those who lived according to *Logos* (according to Reason) are Christians, even if they were thought to be atheists, as among the Greeks Socrates. For Christ was partially known even by Socrates, for He was and is the *Logos* who is in every man, as a power of the ineffable Father and not the mere instrument of human reason."

Fourteen hundred years later, Erasmus, in this same tradition, would exclaim, "Saint Socrates, pray for us!"

This historically crucial equation of the *Logos* with Christ changes the *Logos* more than it changes Christ. Justin did not turn the Christian religion into Platonic philosophy; he found the fulfillment of Platonic philosophy in the Christian religion. Like John, when Justin made the equation it didn't change what Christians meant by Christ—from eternity He had always been the Mind of God, the residence of eternal truth—but it changed what philosophers meant by the *Logos*: it became flesh and spoke to us. *Logos* became *dia-logos*, dialog. Man had always sought for God, and failed, even at his best, in Plato; but when God sought for man, He succeeded, in Christ. Justin's experience was like Job's: Job's words about God failed, and did not satisfy; when God spoke to Job, God's Word succeeded, and satisfied Job. And the reason is the *Logos*. The *Logos* is the heart of Christian Platonism.

When we fast forward to the height of the Christian Middle Ages, the thirteenth century, we find two philosophers, Bonaventure and Aquinas, who exemplified Christian Platonism in very different ways. They were also close personal friends, by the way, and both were canonized saints and doctors of the Church. Bonaventure philosophized in a purely Platonic way, marrying Plato to the spirit of St. Francis of Assisi even when he used the terminology of Aristotle. Aquinas was more Aristotelian in content, but he still regarded Augustine more highly than Aristotle and quoted him more frequently than Aristotle in his *Summa*, even though on some secondary but important technical issues he was more Aristotelian than Augustinian—especially in anthropology, about the relation between body and soul, and in epistemology, about the relation between sensation and reason.

Bonaventure used Aristotelian terminology to make Platonic points. As a matter of fact, just about all medieval philosophers before Ockham thought of themselves as synthesizers of Plato and Aristotle, in different ways.

Bonaventure relied most on Augustine, especially his doctrine of divine illumination of the intellect by the Platonic Ideas in the Mind of God. This doctrine alone, he argued, explains the presence of eternal and necessary truths in the human soul, for the soul is not eternal or necessary. We are not immutable or infallible, yet these Ideas are. Two plus two *must* be four, and events *must* have causes, and goodness must be done and evil avoided. Bonaventure sees the Ideas as exercising a kind of regulative activity on the human mind, like hardware in a computer, as we would say today. The Ideas are not just an abstract logical *explanation* of the data, of the fact that we know eternal truths. They are a *real presence* of the Mind of God to our minds, however veiled that presence may be.

The essence of Bonaventure's whole philosophy is summarized in the title of his most famous little book, *The Itinerary of the Mind's Journey to God*. He sees the whole of creation as rungs on a ladder for the soul's ascent to God. The universe is a Jacob's ladder, a road to God, because it's first a road down from God. The world is a great cathedral, filled with divinely painted pictures to teach us step by step our own nature and destiny. Everything on earth is an *image*, a resemblance, a sign, a word that expresses a meaning beyond it. Creatures are *words*, God's creating was a *speaking*, and the universe is a *book* on which, he says, we read the Trinity on every page. When our eyes are opened, we see God everywhere, because He *is* everywhere, as an author is everywhere in his book. The four best words to summarize Bonaventure's philosophy might be these: *All things are signs*. It is a very Franciscan sensibility. Think of St. Francis's famous Canticle of the Sun, or, more properly, the Canticle of the Creatures. St. Bonaventure is St. Francis become a philosopher.

Semiotics is the modern science of signs. Walker Percy, the twentieth-century Pulitzer Prize-winning novelist, found semiotics his main path out of materialism, nihilism, and atheism. If you want to understand the importance of Bonaventure's doctrine that things are signs, read Percy's very readable essays, especially *The Message in the Bottle* and *Lost in the Cosmos*.

In Bonaventure the ascent to God, which is the whole meaning of our life, has three stages. First is seeing and loving God in the *vestiges* He has left in matter, which are the *objects* of our souls' knowing and loving—the material things in the world. Second is doing the same in our own souls, made in the *image* of God as *subjects*, that is, as knowers and lovers of these objects. The third way is seeing and loving God finally as God Himself above our souls as the One who *knows* our soul which knows things, and who *loves* our soul, which loves things, because He knew and loved our souls into existence when He created them in His own image as knowers and lovers.

Aquinas was more of an Aristotelian than Bonaventure, who totally followed Augustine's Christian Platonism even when he used Aristotle's vocabulary. Aquinas was *more* than an Augustinian, but not less. Almost never does he simply disagree with

Augustine, but adds Aristotelian vegetables to the Augustinian to make an integrated Plato-Aristotle-Augustine stew.

Where this is most clear and most important is in his metaphysics, especially concerning the central doctrine of all of Platonism, the theory of Ideas.

Aquinas *accepts* Plato's Ideas, and says so explicitly. His only rejection of Plato's metaphysics is the same as Aristotle's: a rejection of their "separation," their aloneness, their independent substantiality. They exist, but not in themselves; they exist in three places, says Aquinas, "before things, in things, and after things": before things as divine Ideas, in things as Aristotelian forms, and after things as human concepts.

In the first place they exist before all things as Platonic Ideas in the mind of God. Here he adds to Plato in two important ways.

First, like Augustine, he gives Plato's Ideas a home in the mind of God. In fact, he explicitly quotes Augustine on this, with approval. So if all red things ceased to exist, the Idea of red would still exist in the mind of God. Here, for Aquinas as well as Augustine, Plato is right and Aristotle is wrong.

His second addition to Plato is that there are Ideas of individuals as well as of universals. Each person, each blade of grass, each subatomic particle, is known by God eternally, before it is created. This is really *more* Platonic than Platonism, not less.

The second place the Platonic Ideas exist is in things, as the forms of material substances, just as Aristotle said. Aquinas adds to Platonism an Aristotelian hylomorphism (matter and form together constitute things, or "substances", as Aristotle calls them). So for Aquinas, without ceasing to be Ideas, they are also forms. It is the *same* Form in the Mind of God and in things. That's why things have order and intelligibility.

Third, they exist in our minds as universal concepts. And here Aquinas adds the Aristotelian doctrine of abstraction to the Augustinian theory of divine illumination to explain how these eternal Forms get into our temporal minds: God put them into things and we abstract them from material things with our active intellect so that they can be received into our passive or receptive intellect. They can't enter our immaterial intellect when they're united to matter, somewhat as a man can't take his wife with him into the men's room or as we can't take our gold with us to Heaven.

But even here Aquinas does not reject Augustine and his Platonic epistemology of divine illumination, but synthesizes it with Aristotle's epistemology of abstraction. Our "active intellect," which abstracts the form from the matter, is our participation in, and the effect of, God's intellect. So Aristotelian "abstraction" is the effect of Augustinian "illuminations. He says that the divine Mind, the *Logos*, is the first cause of all human intellection just as it is the first cause of the existence of material things. It illuminates us from within rather than from without, and unconsciously rather than consciously, and by nature rather than by supernatural grace; but that's all true for Augustine too. Augustine just didn't know the Aristotelian epistemology of abstraction. Again, Aquinas adds to Augustine, as Augustine added to Plato, rather than subtracting.

Another way Aquinas is a Platonist is in his hermeneutics. Hermeneutics is the science of interpretation, and this means two things: interpreting the real things and events in the world, and interpreting words and texts, especially sacred texts. As we saw with Bonaventure, the medievals typically applied hermeneutics to things and events as well as texts, because they saw the things in the world as signs, written by God, and meant to be read, like a book: the "book of nature." They developed the ancient and largely forgotten art of sign reading. Everything earthly was an image of something heavenly; everything in the creation was a reflection of something in the Creator. Remember, God wrote *two* books, nature and scripture. Both were meant to be read, looked-along rather than just looked-at. That reading raises us above the animals. Somebody who can't sign-read the book of nature is like a dumb dog who only looks at your finger when you point to where you want him to go instead of reading the sign and looking *along* your finger so as to understand your mind, your will, your intentions. Animals deal very well with matter, but they can't understand that matter reveals spirit. That's why God *invented* matter in the first place: to be an image of His spirit, His Ideas, of Platonic Ideas, of the *Logos*; to make the *Logos* flesh in a million impersonal ways before It became flesh personally in Christ. The universe is a kind of appetizer for the Incarnation.

This is not just in Justin and Augustine and Bonaventure but also Aquinas. Aquinas wrote a long commentary on John's Gospel using Augustine's Platonic interpretation of the *Logos*.

Aquinas applies this idea that nature as well as scripture is full of *signs* when he explains the   philosophical foundation for the medieval fourfold method of exegesis, which justifies interpreting scripture as both literal and symbolic. This is not just Aquinas; it's typical of the Middle Ages, and Aquinas is just the most famous exponent of it. It says there are four possible right interpretations of the person and events in scripture.

It's the narrative books, the historical events, that are the most important part of scripture. All the wisdom literature and all the prophetic literature is secondary to the narrative, the story line, both in the Jewish and in the Christian scriptures, unlike the scriptures of all other world religions. And these events are to be interpreted, first of all, literally and historically: they really happened. But they are also to be interpreted symbolically, as signs pointing beyond themselves to other things, in three ways.

First, the events in the Old Testament point forward Messianically, to their fulfillment in the New Testament. For instance, Moses is Moses but also a symbol of Christ, Pharaoh also symbolizes the Devil, the exodus from Egypt symbolizes salvation, the crossing of the Red Sea symbolizes the conquest of death, the wilderness symbolizes purgatory, the promised land symbolizes heaven, and the old law, given from Mount Sinai, symbolizes the new law, the Gospel, given by Christ.

A second symbolic interpretation is that the persons and events in the story symbolize aspects of ourselves and our present lives: *our* Peter first confesses Christ, then abandons Him; *our* Judas betrays him; *our* Mary conceives Him by faith and baptism, and so on.

Third, the events also symbolize future, heavenly events. For instance, Jesus heals physical blindness, and that symbolizes the healing of our mental and spiritual blindness in the Beatific Vision in heaven.

It's not so much the fourfold method itself but Aquinas's philosophical justification of it that shows his deep Platonic mindset. He says that man can only write with words, but God also writes with events, and that is why events can rightly be seen as words, as *signs* and not just things.

That most recent and most radical philosophy called Deconstructionism centers on the denial that even words are signs, and reduces them to things that are either the causes or effects of power. The Platonic tradition, exemplified by Aquinas's hermeneutic, is the total opposite of this because it says that even things are words and signs as well as being things. Premodernist Platonism gets you out of the cave and shows you that everything is more than it seems to be. Postmodernist Deconstructionism tells you that even the handwriting on the wall of your cave is less than it seems, that your assumption that at least *words* are meaningful is wrong, so that your world is much *less* than you think it is. That's the fundamental issue: are there *more* things, even more *kinds* of things, in heaven and earth than are dreamed of in our philosophy, in our ideas, as Platonism says, or just the same things, or less? Is reality more than the cave, just the cave, or less than the cave?

Aquinas holds together the different kinds of symbolism, and holds together the symbolic and the literal, by his doctrine of *analogy*.

A symbol is a kind of analogy in words, of course, but for Aquinas analogies are not just in words and language or just in thought and concepts, but they are first of all in being. Reality itself is analogical. The reality that we designate by the word "good" when we predicate that word of God, a man, a dog, a medicine, a theory, and a weapon, is six different but related realities. A good man is not just an affectionate pet, and a good dog does not make free choices. A good medicine heals, but a good weapon kills. And all these other things *have* goodness, have *some* goodness, but God *is* goodness, *all* goodness. The Form of Goodness is not univocal, like a number, with one fixed and unchanging meaning only, but it is analogical: partly the same and partly different as it moves through the different levels of reality.

Being itself is analogical for Aquinas, for God *is* being while all creatures only *have* being. God's essence is to exist, but creatures need existence added to their essence. That's why horses are real but unicorns are not, even though the essence of a unicorn is just as possible as the essence of a horse: it's only existence that makes an essence actual as well as possible. A square circle is neither possible nor actual; a unicorn is possible but not actual; a horse is both possible and actual; and God alone is purely actual, not possible but necessary. A square circle has neither essence nor existence. A unicorn has essence but no existence. A horse has both essence and existence, because God gives existence to its essence by creating it. And God is pure existence; without any additional limiting, finite essence, as in a horse: His essence *is* unlimited existence.

This Thomistic distinction between essence and existence was a crucial metaphysical addition to Plato's theory of Forms, and it came from the Biblical revelation of creation. That the one God created the very existence of everything else than Himself out of nothing is a purely Jewish idea, an idea that no pagan ever thought of. This is not Platonism. For Plato, all the essences are actual eternally; for Aquinas, God chooses to actualize only some possible essences in creating them, in giving them existence. But all possible Forms or essences exist eternally in His mind, both for Plato and for Aquinas, so Aquinas is not subtracting anything from Plato, but adding the notion of existence to what Plato said about essence.

Plato has in every age been the Christian philosopher's first friend, even when Aristotle became the second. The thirteenth century's rediscovery of Aristotle had to be prepared for twelve centuries of Platonism, just as Aristotle himself had to have the broad shoulders of Plato to stand on. (By the way the name "Plato" *means* "broad shoulders." When he was young Plato was reputed to have been a wrestler.)

Let's move from Aquinas' metaphysics to his anthropology: how is Plato present there?

Even though he is an Aristotelian, Aquinas also accepts the three most important theses of Plato's anthropology:

First, the most important part of you is your soul, and the most important thing in life is the care of the soul (and Aristotle agreed with this even though he added the body much more than Plato did).

Second, the soul is immortal, which Aristotle denied.

Third, the soul must be a substance, as Plato said, because if it were only the form of the body, as Aristotle said, then it could not be immortal. (Actually, Aristotle fudges a bit on immortality, and Aquinas interprets him very charitably, probably too charitably, as making possible room for immorality.)

Aquinas says that the soul is both a substance in itself, so that it can exist in itself, *and* designed to be the form of the body, so that it its identity is incomplete without a body. By saying both these things, the Platonic thing and the Aristotelian thing, Aquinas preserves both the possibility of immortality and the psychosomatic unity. Once again, it is a synthesis of Plato and Aristotle, not simply Aristotle versus Plato.

Just as with the doctrine of the Platonic Ideas, Aquinas rejects not the primary Platonic point but the secondary point about its *relationship* to other things. Aquinas follows Aristotle in relating the soul more closely to the body than Plato did, just as he follows Aristotle in relating form more closely to matter, Ideas more closely to things, than Plato did. But even Plato had the Ideas related to things by "participation": things "participate" in their Forms. This idea of "participation" has been neglected by historians of philosophy who traditionally paint a simple contrast between Plato and Aristotle. "Participation" is one of the most often—occurring terms and one of the most important connecting concepts throughout Aquinas's philosophy, as it was for Plato.

But the relationship is more than just participation in Aristotle and Aquinas: it's matter and form constituting one substance, the hylomorpic unity, in metaphysics; and body and soul constituting one substance, the psychosomatic unity, in anthropology.

In Aquinas's anthropology, the soul is real, and immortal, and substantial, just as Plato said, but the body is not merely its temporary hotel, "this old house," or its prison cell, as Plato said.

Here, as everywhere, it's Aquinas' instinct to synthesize, to add to Plato but not to subtract from him except where Plato himself subtracted from reality, as he did in treating the body so lightly.

Lecture V:
Nominalism

We saw, in our last lecture, that even when Christian philosophers like Justin and Bonaventure and Aquinas added to Plato, they started with him. And these corrections of Plato, especially by taking the body more seriously, were done in the spirit of Plato; I mean by that that they were "mores," not "lesses," more steps leading us out of the little cave and into a bigger world.

That's what education means, literally, "leading out." The whole history of philosophy can be an education in cave exiting. Or, alternatively, it can also lead us down into smaller and smaller caves, into crevasses in the ground. Because moving around in our cave, exploring—in other words, education—is a *dangerous* thing, and it can lead us out of light into darkness as well as out of darkness into light. In this lecture and in the next two we will explore three forms of that darkness and littleness by which modern thinkers contracted Platonism instead of expanding it, as the Christian Platonists did: first Nominalism, then Positivism, or Reductionism, and then finally Nihilism.

These are three results of the rejection of Platonism in three areas of modern and contemporary philosophy, and all three have proved to be not merely problematic but disastrous. Nominalism has proved a disaster for theoretical philosophy, especially in metaphysics; Positivism and Reductionism has undermined methodology in all philosophy, especially in epistemology; and Nihilism has undermined practical philosophy, philosophy of values, or ethics.

Finally, in our last lecture, I will point to some chinks in the confining walls of the cave, some hopeful signs that even in our anti-Platonic age, we are still able to escape the little caves that our anti-Platonic philosophers want to confine us in, not so much in technical philosophy as in everyday life.

So let's begin with Nominalism. What is it and why is it so destructive?

If I were to select just one philosophy and one philosopher to blame for most of the mistakes of modern philosophy, and the most *foundational* mistakes, I would select Nominalism and blame William of Ockham. I call him a home-wrecker, or a marriage-wrecker. Not only did he put an end to the fundamental program of one thousand four hundred years of Christian philosophy, which was the marriage or synthesis of faith and reason, but within philosophy itself his Nominalism divided what had previously been happily married or united, in every philosophical area: universals and particulars, concepts and their objects, certainty and reality, terms and propositions, consciousness and the world, and the two terms of every analogy. With just one idea—Nominalism—he marched through all the areas of philosophy like a sword destroying all these unions. And the root of all of them is a single one: his mercilessly eradication of all traces of Platonism, that is, of *Logos*, of a real cosmic order of universal Forms, natures, or essences.

This is a very severe judgment, but I shall try to prove it.

Nominalism is an answer to a simple question in logic: What is the reality that abstract universal terms like justice or redness or human nature refer to? Sounds like a harmless question about some very abstract idea, but (to quote the very quotable title of an old book) "ideas have consequences."

To understand the question, we have to review some basic logic. Logic is essentially the science of reasoning. Reasoning is the act of the mind by which we prove one proposition to be true (called the conclusion), by deducing it from other propositions (called premises). That's called an *argument*. Both the premises and conclusions in an argument are *propositions*, and propositions are declarative sentences.

Now just as an argument is composed of propositions, the premises and the conclusion, so a proposition is composed of two *terms*, the subject and the predicate. For instance, in the classic argument "All men are mortal, and Socrates is a man, therefore Socrates is mortal," the whole thing is the argument, and it is logically valid because the conclusion is proved by the premises, its truth logically follows from the truth of the premises. The conclusion is "Socrates is mortal" and the premises are "All men are mortal and Socrates is a man." Both premises are true; and since the conclusion follows from them, we know the conclusion is therefore true.

Those are two of the three check points of any argument. The third check point is the terms. "Mortal" is one of the terms in both of the premises. If all the terms are clear and unambiguous, they pass their logical check point, and if all the premises are true, they pass their logical check point, and if the argument is logically valid (if the conclusion necessarily fallows from the premises), it passes its logical check point; and if the argument passes all three check points, we know its conclusion must be true.

Now let's focus on the terms, because that's where Nominalism comes in. There are three kinds of terms. Terms can be either *singular*, referring to only one concrete thing, like Socrates; or *particular*, referring some members of a class, like "Some men will die today"; or *universal*, referring to the class of such and thus to all members of the class, like "All men are mortal." Now Nominalism is an answer to the question, what realities do these universal terms refer to? What are we talking about when we say all men are mortal?

Some propositions have nothing but singular terms in both subject and predicate, like "This man is Socrates," and it is very clear what these two terms refer to. But some propositions have universal predicates, like "Socrates is human"; and some have universal subjects, like "Justice is a virtue"; and some have universal subjects *and* universal predicates, like "all men are mortal." What reality do these universal terms refer to?

Nominalism's simple answer is: nothing. (Nominalism always gives simple answers—it is a form of Reductionism, reducing something more to something less.) According to

Nominalism, universality exists only in terms, in names, in *nomina*, not in reality. According to Nominalism, there is no such thing as human nature, or the nature of man, or man in general; there is only Socrates and Plato. There is no such thing in reality as justice or injustice, only acts that we see as resembling each other in some way so that we choose to use the same term, "just" or "unjust", to refer to them. "Everything outside the soul is singular"— that is the formula for Ockham's Nominalism. Only singular terms designate realities. Nothing is universal except our use of terms.

From this simple premise many radical conclusions follow. Ockham logically and ruthlessly follows them all out, however radical and destructive they are. Here are some of the conclusions Ockham himself draws from his Nominalism.

First, and most important for medieval philosophy, is that theology is not a science. Religious faith is irrational. Reason cannot prove God's existence, since there are no universal premises like "All events require causes" from which we can deduce the existence of God as the First Cause. Reason is too weak to do that. Faith and reason cannot be married, because Reason is too small, too young to have intercourse with Faith. They can't have children.

In Ockham's theology, God Himself is totally irrational: There are no universal rules for the divine mind. God is pure will, and totally free, beyond the universal bounds even of logic. Ockham says that God, being omnipotent, could do anything. He could make a square circle. He could make a man a donkey—not just make a man *turn into* a donkey, but make a man *to be* a donkey even though he is a man. He says that God could cause the sense experience of a star to exist in us when the star does not exist. He is really denying secondary causality. He's dividing the real world into totally separate things and events and saying that it could be that God causes each thing or event separately rather than having one thing cause another according to certain universal laws. So we can't know any universal laws at all. God could make the past not to have been, and He could cause us to remember yesterday when yesterday did not exist because he could have created the universe this morning, with all its fossils and memories already in it. (The anti-evolutionary fundamentalists should latch onto that idea: God created million-year-old dinosaur fossils six thousand years ago just to test the faith of the skeptical scientists.) For Ockham's God is all will and no reason. There are no divine Ideas. Everything is dependent on God's will and nothing else for its intelligibility. God's primary attribute is not wisdom or goodness or love but power, omnipotence.

As we shall see later, this is precisely the crisis in Muslim theology that happened five centuries before Ockham: The Asharites, who embraced Nominalism, Irrationalism, and Voluntarism (will instead of reason) become main-line orthodoxy in Muslim theology. But Nominalism was seen as an aberration in most Christian thought.

Another radical consequence of Nominalism is skepticism. Certainty is impossible, only probability is possible. Nominalism obviously entails skepticism, or at least probablism, because if there are no real universals, then no universal statements can be known to be true of objective reality. And without a universal premise, there can be no valid deductive argument, only probable inductive arguments from singular premises, increasing in probability as you increase the number of premises, or examples, but never reaching certainty because you never reach the universal.

A more technical logical reason for skepticism in Ockham is his point that only the formal logical law of non-contradiction can ever prove that anything is distinct from anything else. You can know that a dog is not a non-dog just as you can know that X is not non-X, but you can't know that a dog is not a god by reason, only by faith.

Still another reason for to skepticism, at least of ordinary knowledge and ordinary reasoning, such as reasoning the existence of God from the degrees of perfection in the universe, or the argument from design to Designer, on the analogy of the human artist, is that there is no real analogy; everything is zero-sum, like numbers. Ockham's logic is strictly mathematical logic, not the

Aristotelian logic of ordinary language, where words have analogical meanings, rubber meanings that stretch, meanings that are not wholly the same and not wholly different, e.g. the goodness of God, of man, of animals, of tools, and of ideas. The word "good" is not wholly the same in all those cases, but it's not wholly different either. But for Ockham every meaningful word is either totally the same or totally different, either univocal, like "three" in three trees and three cats, or equivocal, like "pen" in an ink pen and a pig pen, or "bark" in a dog's bark and a tree's bark. As two is wholly different from three, every term is either wholly the same or wholly different from every other term in Ockham's logic. That's the nature of mathematical logic as distinct from Aristotelian logic, which is the logic of ordinary language.

Another way Ockham makes this same point is by saying that one reality can never be the basis for several concepts; every difference in concepts points to different realities. As Descartes would say two centuries later, every idea must be a clear and distinct idea. Like numbers. Thus Ockham says that the only real unity is numerical unity. Therefore there can be no such thing as the unity of the human race in common humanity. Since there is no such thing as universal human nature, there is no real universal human community. The same is true of the church or a family. They are only relationships between individuals. There is no such real thing as a community, a common unity of diverse yet unified parts, either among men or among the things in the universe. There is no such thing as cosmic order. Because there is no *Logos*. Platonism is dead.

Next, real causality is denied. Ockham reduces causality to sensory observation that one thing regularly follows another, exactly as David Hume was to do four centuries later. Causality is nothing real, only mental: observed sequence, the mental habit of expecting one thing to follow another again merely because we've seen it happen many times before. Eggs just follow birds, we can't know they are caused by birds. Maybe God causes the egg instead of the bird causing it. We can't know that.

Ockham is most famous for the principle called "Ockham's Razor," which states that the simplest explanation is always to be preferred. The principle is a good practical principle for judging alternative scientific hypotheses—you don't want to bring in angels and devils to explain history, or immortal souls when you do brain chemistry—but as a principle in theoretical philosophy it means Reductionism. Deny everything you possibly can deny. Ockham applied the razor not just to the extra hair on philosophy's beard but to its neck, its jugular vein. The Razor is his justification for Nominalism, the denial of essences, natures, species, or universals.

In epistemology the consequence is the denial of abstraction. Since there are no universals there is no abstracting of them, and therefore there is no need for an active intellect to do the abstracting. The intellect is purely passive, like a blank tablet, a "tabula rasa," simply receiving data from the senses as a blackboard receives lines from chalk. All the activity is in the chalk.

In ethics, Ockham totally severs ethics from metaphysics—goodness from reality—in denying natural law. Natural law has to be universal: universal rights presuppose universal natures: we have human rights because we are all human. For Ockham, since there is no real universal human nature, morality is not based on human nature and the virtues that perfect it, but purely on our obligation to obey God's arbitrary will, as in mainline Islamic thought. Morality is reduced to jurisprudence and legalism, without reasons. Do it because it's commanded, not because it's right. Goodness is nothing but conformity to the will of the lawmaker. Ockham's ethics is essentially that of Thrasymachus and the Sophists, who say that a thing is good only because the human lawmaker willed it, or of Euthyphro, in Plato's dialog by that name, who says that a thing is good only because the gods will it. Ockham says that if God willed us to hate Him, or to hate our fellow human being, then hate would be good and love would be evil. Ockham actually says that. This is exactly the philosophy of Islamic terrorists.

Here are some of the consequences of Ockham's Nominalism in modern philosophy.

Modern philosophy really begins in the early seventeenth century with Francis Bacon's Empiricism and Rene Descartes' Rationalism. These are the two essential parts of the new scientific method: reducing all data to empirical data by insisting on empirical proof for every hypothesis, and reducing all reason to mathematical reason by insisting on exact mathematical measurement and the closest thing to it outside of numbers, viz. "clear and distinct ideas." This tighter method made for great success in science. But Bacon and Descartes made these principles into methods for philosophy too.

Nominalism obviously leads to Empiricism, which means reducing all valid knowledge to sensory knowledge, reducing reason to "the scout for the senses," as Hobbes says. The reason for this reduction of reason is that the senses see particulars and the reason knows universals, and if there *are* no universals, there is nothing left for the reason to do but aid the senses.

Within reason, Nominalism reduces reason to mathematics, which happens in Descartes. Descartes insists that all ideas be "clear and distinct ideas," like numbers. The method can't handle analogical ideas, "stretch" ideas, ideas with edges that stretch to connect with other ideas in a "more or less" kind of way. The ideal is always mathematics. You could say that Bacon reduced the mind to a camera and Descartes to a computer.

David Hume, a century after Bacon and Descartes, is probably the most famous skeptic in history, and certainly the most influential in philosophy. His Nominalism, inherited from Ockham, led to skepticism by a very clear logical route. Hume argues that every proposition must be either what he calls a "relation of ideas" or a "matter of fact." A relation of ideas is a tautology, provable by the law of non contradiction alone, like $2 + 2 = 4$. A matter of fact is something that happens in the world of matter, time, and space, and it's uncertain until you observe it with your senses. You have seen the sun rise yesterday but you have not seen the sun rise tomorrow, and since all knowledge comes through the senses, you can't know that the sun will rise tomorrow. You can't deduce that from a universal, like "the sun rises every day" because there are no universals. All you can know is sensations, not universal laws, and therefore nothing future. You can't even know that nature will always act in a uniform way. A dropped stone tomorrow may fly up into the sky for no discernible reason; you can't know whether it will or not until you try it and see it. All you can know is what you have seen: that in the past these things have not yet happened. You can't know that the future will resemble the past because there is no such thing as a common nature, a universal.

It all stems from his principle about only two kinds of propositions, tautologies and sense observations. Neither of these two kinds of propositions gives you *Logos*, real essences, Platonic Forms. Once again, it is Platonism that is the central dividing point.

Let's look at the logic here a little more carefully, since Nominalism arose as a doctrine about logic and language. I know this is dull and abstract, but it's the foundation for radically important practical consequences that are exciting—or terrifying.

A proposition joins a predicate term to a subject term. It either asserts or denies that the predicate is true of the subject. For instance, "Socrates was fat," or "Socrates was not fat." Traditional, commonsensical, ordinary language logic, which was first formulated by Aristotle, says there are five possible relationships between any predicate and its subject, five different aspects of the subject that the predicate may reveal. For instance, "Man is a rational animal" reveals the *species* or essential nature or essence of man. "Man is an animal" reveals the *genus*, the general aspect of the essence, the aspect man shares with other things, like apes and worms and lawyers. "Man is rational" reveals the *specific difference*, the specific aspect of the essence, the aspect that distinguishes man from other animals, other members of the same genus. "Some men are bald" reveals an *accident* of the subject, because baldness is accidental to the essence of man. If a man is bald, it's by accident, not by essence. Finally, "Man has a sense of humor" or "Man has language" reveals a *property, proper accident,* or *essential property* of man: not the very essence but something that flows from the essence, is caused by the essence, and therefore is there in every man.

Now if there are no essences, there are no essential properties. All properties are accidents. And if there are no essences, then genus, species, and specific difference are only our invented conventions of language. We have chosen to label man as an animal, so that "Man is an animal" becomes a tautology. It tells you nothing about the real world, only about the relation between the two words in our labelling system.

There's no room in Hume for essential properties, because they "flow from" or follow from, the essence and we can understand this "following from the essence" only because we can understand the essence; We understand that all men are mortal because we understand human nature, the universal essence, as containing an animal body, an organism, and we understand an organism as a body that can die if and when its interdependent organs stop working. But for a Nominalist there is no such thing as understanding an essence, because there are no essences.

So you can't be sure that all men are mortal, and therefore you can't be sure that you are mortal. Because you can't know the essence of human nature, you can't deduce mortality from your understanding of animality. You don't really understand anything, any essential natures, because there are no essential natures to understand. You are simply a camera plus a computer with a dictionary in it. All meaningful propositions, for Hume, are either tautologies or accidental.

Hume famously expressed his skepticism when he wrote:

"When we run over to libraries persuaded of these principles, what havoc must we make? If we take into our hands any volume of theology or metaphysics, for example, let us ask: Does it contain any reasoning about quantity or number? No. Does it contain any information about matters of fact and existence (i.e. observable existing things)? No. Commit it then to the flames, for it can contain nothing but sophistry and illusion."

Immanuel Kant, the most influential philosopher of modern times, wrote, "David Hume awoke me from my dogmatic slumber." Kant thought that to save human knowledge he had to answer Hume. But instead of doing this by going back to Plato and Aristotle and universals, Kant accepted Ockham's Nominalism and within that narrow confine he answered Hume's skepticism in a new way: by what he called his "Copernican Revolution in philosophy."

Both Rationalists, like Descartes, whom Kant called "dogmatic," and Empiricists, whom Kant called "skeptical," shared a common false assumption, Kant thought. He was right there: the common false assumption was Nominalism. But Kant identified the common false assumption as epistemological realism, the common sense notion that truth means the conformity of thinking to objective reality, the notion that our thought can and should mirror its real object. Kant reversed this assumption and maintained that objects mirror our thought. We see things in time and space not because they really are in time and space but because time and space are the forms we all have to impose on things in the act of sensing them. The abstract logical categories like causality and substance and relation are also subjective to the mind, but present in all minds: they are the way everyone has to think, but we cannot know that they are the ways in which things actually exist and behave. Causality is how we think the world, not how the world really is. Finally, even the concepts of God, a self, and a world, are what Kant called "ideas of pure reason," which we all unconsciously impose on everything we think to order it. All order comes from the mind. All human thought is like art, not like science; it creates order rather than discovering it. There are no real universals, we just make them up. But we all make them up in the same way, and we have to; there's no other way we can think.

This seems to me to be an even more radical skepticism than Hume's, because Kant says that we can never know "things in themselves," or objective reality, at all. We can only know that it exists, because *something* impinges on our senses and our consciousness and activates it, but we can know nothing about what it is. "What it is," you see, is the formula for a Platonic Idea, a universal; and we cannot know any real universals, according to Nominalism.

When I think of Kant's Copernican Revolution I'm haunted by a cartoon of two castaways on a desert island. A bottle washes up with a message in it, and there's hope on their faces as they retrieve it from the sea. But the hope disappears when they read the message. The caption says; "It's only from ourselves." That's Kant's message: that all the logos, all the messages that seem to come to us from a world outside ourselves are only coming from ourselves. I'm terrified by this because that's what I think Hell is: the falling away of all otherness, so that you are left only with yourself. There's no real other to know and love. That's Hell: you've rejected God, and death takes the universe away from you, so the only thing left to you, forever, is yourself. You're the worm endlessly chewing on its own tail. Personally, I'd rather have some demons with pitchforks to fight against than that.

To be fair to Kant, he says that we do have a common mind, which he calls the "transcendental ego" as well as our individual mind, which he calls "the empirical ego," so we're not lonely egos. But this common mind isn't the community of real other individual persons, it just seems to be a kind of pantheistic tapioca pudding, and we find ourselves to be only lumps in the tapioca. (That's C. S. Lewis's image.)

And all this, all these terrifying existential consequences, stem from Nominalism, which is the denial of Plato's Big Idea. Even in its denial, Platonism proves to be the central key to Western philosophy.

Much of twentieth-century philosophy is a logical and linguistic application of Hume. Philosophy departments in almost all English speaking universities in the last half of the twentieth century found themselves in a war between the traditionalists, who wanted to keep doing philosophy in the old Socratic-Platonic-Aristotelian way, and the new so-called "analytic philosophers," who pretty much gave up on the entire history of Western philosophy except for Hume, and said that philosophy's job is not to discover truth but to analyze logic and language. These philosophy wars are not wholly over, but almost, because many philosophers have found ways to combine the new and the old, to use the new logic to ask the old questions, even questions of metaphysics, instead of just dismissing it all as sophistry and illusion, as Hume did. They are not necessarily Nominalists.

What holds analytic philosophers together then? Mainly the use of the new symbolic or mathematical or propositional logic instead of the old Socratic-Platonic-Aristotelian logic. But the essential difference between the two logics is still about Nominalism, because the new logic is called propositional logic because it begins with propositions whereas the old logic begins with terms, including universal terms, which have to be defined, and real definitions express universal essences. And these terms are then related in propositions not just in Hume's two ways, as tautologies or accidental propositions, but in Aristotle's five ways that we went over before: genus, species, difference, property, and accident, the five predicables. Aristotelian logic applies to the understanding of universal essences, essential natures.

But mathematical logic or propositional logic does not. It is the logic of computers. Computers are nominalistic; they don't understand any essences at all. They are just very, very fast and accurate calculators. And digital computers have *no* understanding of analogies, and we are becoming more like them. That's why the people who design the SAT tests, the college entrance exams, totally dropped the analogy section a decade ago; no one could pass it any more.

All forms of skepticism are self-contradictory, because, as Wittgenstein said, "to draw a limit to thought you must think both sides of the limit." Thus the skeptic has to say, "It is true that there is no truth. It is certain that there is no certainty. It is objectively true that truth is not objective. I know that I cannot know. It is only probable that there is only probability. There are absolutely no absolutes. It is a universal truth that no truth is universal," et cetera. The skeptic always has the problem of having to be skeptical about his skepticism, like Socrates.

But Nominalism is a form of skepticism. And it's self-contradictory. It announces, as a universal truth, that there are no universals. You can't *say* it without contradicting it. To say "All rivers are totally different" you have to call them all "rivers" and you couldn't do that if they were totally different. You can't say "all" if there are no "all"s. You can't even say "There are no alls" if there are no alls, because to say, "There are no alls," is also to say, "All things lack Allness."

Since Platonism is centrally the doctrine that universals are real, and since the alternative to Platonism is Nominalism, and since Nominalism entails skepticism, there are only two alternatives: Platonism or skepticism. And skepticism is self-contradictory. Thus "Plato is philosophy, and philosophy is Plato," as Emerson said.

But skepticism, and the Nominalism that implies it, is attractive to Irrationalists and anti-intellectuals. For instance, mainline Islam, the source of 90 percent of all the wars in the world today, stems from the Nominalism and skepticism of the Asharites or Mutakalimoun in the ninth century, the fideists or faith-alone people, who got the political power to establish themselves against their theological opponents the Mutazalites, the both-faith-and-reason people. The Mutazalites believed in an Allah who was rational and just, not pure arbitrary power, and therefore believed in universal truths and universal human nature and universal human rights and natural law, both moral and physical. The contempt for reason shown by so much of mainline Islam today stems from the triumph of a Nominalist theology devoid of universals and therefore devoid of reason, a theology of an arbitrary, irrational Allah of pure will, pure force, who magically and miraculously and unilaterally does everything Himself without using or establishing any secondary causes, any universal natural laws, either in ethics or in physics. That is the source of what Robert Reilly calls "the closing of the Muslim mind," in an excellent book by that title. It all goes back to Plato's question in the *Euthyphro*: is a thing good simply because the god wills it, or does the god will it because it is good? C. S. Lewis' old Professor was right: It's all in Plato, all in Plato: bless me, what *do* they teach them at these schools?

The roots of most wars, past and present, lie in philosophy, ultimately in metaphysics, in one's concept of ultimate reality. If you want to be a practical politician and successful international policy maker, you must study philosophy.

Islam is a very clear example of that today.

Most Muslims in the West believe in peace, justice, and universal human rights, and condemn terrorism; and there are many passages in the Koran that teach that. But we also find the opposite, especially in the Wahhabi school. The ultimate source of Islamic terrorism is the rejection of the Platonic tradition, of *Logos*, or universal rationality.

The connection is clear: If God is irrational, then it is wrong for us to use reason, to philosophize, especially in theology. The Koran must then be simply recited and memorized, not understood or reasoned about. The Asharite school declared it heresy to believe that the Koran was created in time as a way for Allah to condescend to the level of man's reason, and to believe that there was such a thing as universal reason, and therefore universal human rights, human dignity, and, sometimes, even human free will—which made democracy impossible, for those are its fundamental philosophical foundations.

At the other side in the ninth-century debate from the Asharites, Averroes demoted faith almost as much as his opponents demoted reason. The crisis both sides faced was the apparent contradictions between the Koran and Aristotle, the greatest of philosophers, who denied individual immortality, the creation of the world of time, and divine providence. Averroes taught a kind of double truth theory: that while it was all right for simple people to believe the Koran literally, for educated people and philosophers Aristotle trumped the Koran, and where the two contradicted, the Koran had to be reinterpreted allegorically. So Averroes was like our modern Western secularist Rationalists who demoted faith as much as his opponents, the Asharites, demoted reason. Unfortunately, there was no Muslim Thomas Aquinas to mediate and synthesize faith and reason. There are such Muslim voices today, mostly in the West, and the future of Islam and the lives of many innocent human beings in the next century depend on which brand of this faith triumphs, the one that includes Platonic reason and universality or the one based on anti-Platonic irrationalism that gives birth to blind will and terrorism.

I think this crisis in Islam that stems from Nominalism throws a very useful light on the political crisis of our own *western* civilization and the current "culture wars" between so-called liberals and so-called conservatives in the West. Historically speaking, conservatism and liberalism, or progressivism, are relative terms; yesterday's progressives, once they succeed, become tomorrow's conservatives; and people like myself who used to call ourselves liberals because of our defense of Platonic universal reason and natural law against right-wing fundamentalists who deny them, now have to call ourselves conservatives because we have not changed our opinions at all, but our political situation has changed the labels. The people who now officially deny natural law in law schools and natural reason in humanities departments staffed with Postmodernists call themselves liberals. *Logos* does not change; what changes is the political labels on its defenders and deniers.

Platonic *Logos* helps us to sort out this confusion. From the Platonic point of view, what I would call bad conservatives and bad liberals are really philosophically identical. They are irrationalists, voluntarists, subjectivists, ideologists, fundamentalists, skeptics. The only difference between the bad conservatives and the bad liberals is that the conservatives believe in an irrational, arbitrary *God*, like the Muslim fundamentalists, while the liberals believe in an irrational, arbitrary *humanity*, like the Sophists.

On the other side, what I would call good conservatives and good liberals are really philosophically identical, because they are both apostles of reason, of *Logos*, of universal natural law. Only when we sort out the sides philosophically rather than politically can we tell who our real friends are and who our real enemies are; and it is the Platonic tradition that does that for us.

Lecture VI:
Positivism

In this lecture we'll explore another consequence of the denial of Platonism, namely, Positivism. It's closely connected with Nominalism, and a logical consequence of Nominalism, just as skepticism is, but it's more concerned with values. It might be a useful oversimplification at the start to define Nominalism as the denial of any universal objective truths, and Positivism as the denial of any universal objective values. Values, for Positivism, are contrasted with "Facts" and are not based on *Logos*, on the Platonic kind of reason that knows universals, but on the human will that creates them, that "posits" them. Thus the term "Positivism."

The word "Positivism" was coined by Auguste Comte, the nineteenth-century French atheist philosopher who founded the science of sociology and invented that term. He called his philosophy "Positivism" because he believed that the only knowledge of objective reality was through what he called "positive science." He didn't mean by "positive" the opposite of "negative" but the opposite of "natural." He said that the idea that things really had natures, reflections of Platonic Forms, was a superstition that originated in religion. He said that God, the soul, Platonic Forms, and the afterlife were all "posited" or invented or created by human minds rather than discovered in objective reality. He said that Plato only replaced gods with Forms—for instance, Zeus with Justice, Aphrodite with Beauty, Apollo with Truth, and so on— but that these Forms were simply intellectual and abstract versions of gods. Both were mere myths and superstitions posited or invented by myth-makers, by men. He summarized all human history as passing through three stages: the religious stage, the philosophical stage, and the "positive scientific" stage, which he predicted would soon abolish all religion and all philosophy. He treated this third stage as a new religion, a religion of atheist humanism. He even composed a new atheist liturgy and atheist hymns for his new religion of humanity. My response to those who believe this philosophy is that I think they have too much faith. They've been waiting for religion and philosophy to disappear for the better part of two centuries, and they're still waiting, in faith. I can't help being amazed at the strength of their patience with the present and their enormous faith in the future in the teeth of all the evidence.

Today the term "positivism" is usually used in *legal* terminology to mean the denial of any natural law in ethics, any law higher than man-made, or man-posited laws. This, by the way, is the philosophical assumption in the overwhelming majority of all law schools in America today. It's a denial, but it's usually disguised by positive terms, like "Critical Legal Studies," as Harvard calls it. It's the essential position of the Sophists like Thrasymachus in Plato's *Republic*, without Thrasymachus's unsophisticated clarity and shocking crudity, and it sounds much more civilized than Thrasymachus because it bases law not on power, as he did, but on consensus. But what is consensus but the democratic version of power instead of the monarchical version?

Both the ancient version of Positivism, with the Greek Sophists, and the modern version of it today, in American law schools, share the position that justice, and presumably other moral values as well, is nothing but what we choose to call obedience to the laws that we have posited. There is no higher law, no natural law, no law of universal human nature by which we can justify or condemn man-made laws. It is, in other words, the repudiation of the United Nations' Universal Declaration of Human Rights and of the famous first sentence of the American Declaration of Independence. And that is the position that dominates the universities and the courts in America today.

And even more, in Canada. In the spring of 2010 the Supreme Court of Canada voted 7-2 to legalize group sex orgies between adults and consenting children over 13, and the judge who authored the decision explained in an interview that the justification for it was that all morality is subjective and arbitrary and should not be subject to criminalization. In Canada, "morality" means only sexual morality. They have very strict laws about other things—for instance, speech codes—and it's illegal to hurt anyone's feelings by expressing religious or philosophical criticism, in *words*, of what anyone *does* sexually. So instead of free speech and controlled sex, they have free sex and controlled speech.

In this lecture I want to survey nine different forms of Positivism in modern philosophers: methodological, teleological, epistemological, metaphysical, anthropological, ethical, political, logical, and linguistic Positivism.

What is common to all nine is the rejection of the belief that the traditional object sought in each of these divisions of philosophy is an objective reality, and the acceptance of the belief that it is subjective rather than objective, posited by the will rather than discovered by the reason.

The worldview common to all of these versions of Positivism is a narrowing of the real world. Its news report to us is that Plato's cave is all there is. There is less in reality than in the mind, not more. If Hamlet had been a Positivist he would have told Horatio that there are *fewer* things in heaven and earth than are dreamed of in our philosophies. In a word, Positivism means reductionism: reducing the complex to the simple, the large to the small, the more to the less. I call it "nothing buttery": Thought is nothing but brain chemistry, man is nothing but a clever ape, love is nothing but lust, reasoning is nothing but rationalizing. The essential claim of reductionism is always expressed in words like "nothing but." or "merely" or "simply" or "just." or "only." X is nothing but Y.

The logical problem with any kind of reductionism is that, while it seems to be skeptical and humble, it's really the opposite: it's really very dogmatic and arrogant. For if you claim to know that X is nothing but Y, you are saying that there is *in all reality* no

X that is more than Y; but that means you are claiming to know all of reality. And that's not a humble or skeptical claim at all. For instance if you claim to know that God is nothing but a myth, you are claiming to know that there is in all reality no God that is anything more than a myth, and that is claiming to know all reality. The word for knowledge of all reality is "omniscience," and it is by definition a divine attribute. So if you claim to know for sure that there is no God that is not a myth, you are really claiming to be God, and thus there *is* a God—you—unless *you* are a mere myth. I don't mean that as a serious proof for the existence of God, but I do mean it as a demonstration that reductionism is self-contradictory.

The most innocent form of Positivism is methodological Positivism. Positivism or reductionism as a mere method is often perfectly fine, and necessary in science. The brain surgeon has to treat the patient's brain as a mere computer, and forget that the patient is a human being with intrinsic value, an immortal soul, or anything like that, especially if he knows the patient, because otherwise his mind might wander and his hand might shake. For practical purposes he has to forget the other aspects of his patient and just look at his brain as a machine that needs to be repaired. Here's another example: The scientific historian has to confine himself to scientifically verifiable causes, when for instance he explains the rise of Nazism by German resentment at the Treaty of Versailles, the desperate economic situation in the Great Depression, and the fear of Communism. He can't talk about the ultimate meaning and end of history, or temptations from evil spirits, or divine providence or divine judgment or anything like that, even if he believes these things are real. He has to reduce the complex to the simple, especially the trans-empirical to the empirical, and deal with one dimension at a time.

But this reducing is only a practical method, not a philosophy. The surgeon may still believe his patient has a soul, but he can't operate on that, only on the brain. The historian may still believe in evil spirits, but he can't *prove* their presence in Hitler.

Reductionism as a method is not only right but necessary when you're doing science. But we're talking here about Positivism as a philosophy, not just a method; a theory, not just a practice.

But the fact that it works as a method makes it tempting to erect it into a philosophy. That's essentially what Descartes did, in the book that more than any other began modern philosophy the *Discourse on Method*. In the century before its publication, in 1637, the West had finally gotten clear what the scientific method was, and had begun to use it with tremendous success in all the sciences. Descartes' new philosophical experiment in the *Discourse on Method* was to assume that the scientific method should be used everywhere, including philosophy. That's what he tried to do in this book: define the four common principles of the scientific method in all fields, and then apply it. After he defined the method he gave us three chapters on its application: to ethics, to philosophy and theology, and to physics. He never finished a scientific, purely logical ethics (though Kant claimed to do that one hundred fifty years later) and he only began it in physics, though he promised that if we continued to use it we could literally discover everything that is. He did claim to apply it to philosophy and philosophical theology, and constructed a complete system of philosophy, which he intended to be strictly deductive system, like a mathematical system. Not many philosophers think he succeeded. The questions of philosophy that he claimed to answer with quasi-mathematical certainty, however, are still open and there's almost nobody who still believes his promise that some day they will be closed, that some day we will discover and prove everything there is.

But although most philosophers today no longer believe that Descartes succeeded, almost all of them in his own time agreed with his main point, that we should try to do philosophy by the scientific method. (Pascal was the only major philosopher of Descartes's time who did not get on that bandwagon. I'd call him the first Existentialist.) Most modern philosophers looked to science with envy, as most medieval philosophers looked to theology, as their model and as something superior.

What *is* the scientific method? I'd say that the three most important features of the scientific method are: universal doubt, mathematical measurement, and empirical data. All three, in different ways, seem to lead to Positivism when applied to philosophy.

The first principle of Descartes' method in his *Discourse on Method* is also the first principle of the scientific method: that we should begin *not* by assuming the truth of past science, or philosophy or even common sense, however traditional or accepted or authoritative, but doubt everything, assume nothing. Treat every idea as false until it's proved true. Descartes wants to begin philosophy like this, with universal methodological doubt rather than the way Socrates began, which was with methodological faith, treating an idea as true until it's proved false. (Socrates began by assuming that his interlocutor spoke the truth, then tested it, and usually found it wanting.)

The second principle of the scientific method is measuring everything exactly, quantitatively, mathematically. (That's the criterion of an exact science.) Reduce quality to quantity.

And the third principle is to demand empirical tests, to test all theories by empirical data, not just abstract reasoning. Reduce the abstract to the concrete.

Rationalists like Descartes emphasized the second of these points, quasi-mathematical exactness (what Descartes called "clear and distinct ideas," ideas that were as close to numbers as possible, since every number is totally clear and unambiguous and is also quite distinct from every other number). Empiricists like Bacon and Hobbes emphasized the third point, reducing proof to empirical proof.

(2) The new scientific method, methodological Positivism, was a plus for human knowledge. But it was historically connected with another positivism that was a minus, a subtraction, a reductionism which we could call teleological Positivism because it was about the *telos* or *end* of human knowledge. Bacon and Descartes differed about what was central to their method—

mathematical reasoning or empirical data—but they agreed about universal doubt as their beginning. And they also agreed about a far more important point than their beginning, namely, their ultimate end, their goal, their greatest good, what you might call "the meaning of life," the ultimate purpose and end of all philosophy and science and human life itself. For both schools of early modern philosophy, the Rationalists and the Empiricist, this was "the conquest of nature."

The answer Plato and Aristotle gave to that question was: the knowledge of the truth. But knowledge, said Bacon, is not an end, it is a means. Knowledge is for power. Power is the end. Power over nature, the conquest of nature rather than the contemplation of truth. This is, I believe, the single most important distinctive feature of modern Western civilization: a new *summum bonum*. It is almost impossible to overemphasize how radical this is. C. S. Lewis puts it this way, in *The Abolition of Man*, when he points out that this same new *Summum bonud* was, present in both scientific technology and the *un*scientific technology of magic, which arose at the very same time as modern science and technology, *not* in the Middle Ages but in the scientific Renaissance, in the early modern era. Lewis says that for all premodern civilizations, "the cardinal problem of human life was somehow to conform the soul to objective reality, and the means were wisdom, self-discipline, and virtue. For magic and applied science alike the cardinal problem of human life was to conform objective reality to the wishes of the soul, and the means of technique." William Barrett has a brilliant historical critique of this idea in *The Illusion of Technology*.

If objective reality includes Platonic Ideas, outside the Cave, whether in the mind of God or not, then the meaning of life and our supreme happiness is to know them, to contemplate them, and to structure our lives by them, to conform to these superior ideals. But if objective reality includes only the Cave, it is silly to conform to *that* objective reality, to the rocks and sticks in the Cave. Rather, we want to make that conform to us; we want to change that into a more comfortable place to live. In other words, if we are meant to live out under the open sky, it's silly to try to change the sky; the sky is meant to be enjoyed as it is, to look at it and know it and contemplate it and live by it, to "hitch your wagon to a star." But if we are meant to live in a cave, it's silly to dream of the open sky. Our job is only to make the cave a little more comfortable.

So you see the difference Platonism makes isn't just theoretical and abstract; it changes the whole meaning of life. For Platonism that is the joy and wonder of the child discovering and contemplating the truth. For our culture it is the creature comforts of the senior citizen, golf and luxury cars and good food and medicine. Think of what that means. It means that our civilization is *not* young and vibrant spiritually. It's old and bored. It was classical, premodern civilization that was young. If you want to see what our ancestors looked like, look at a child in Africa. If you want to see what we look like, go live in Florida.

(3) Our third Positivism is epistemological. While premodern philosophy began with and centered on metaphysics, the science of being, modern philosophy begins with and centers on epistemology, the science of knowing. There are three classic answers to the epistemological question in modern philosophy: Rationalism, Empiricism, and Kantianism. All three have in common some kind of reductionism.

Rationalism (Descartes, Spinoza, and Leibnitz) reduces knowledge to clear and distinct ideas. Many history of philosophy textbooks classify Plato as a Rationalist, or Descartes as a Platonist. But there is a significant difference: Plato's ideas are qualitative, not quantitative. Quantitative reasoning is only the third step on Plato's Divided Line in the *Republic*. Above this is the knowledge of the Forms, and above even this is the knowledge of the Good, the absolute. So Plato is not a Cartesian kind of Rationalist. Descartes reduces Plato.

The second modern epistemology, Empiricism (Bacon, Hobbes, Locke, Berkeley and Hume), reduces knowledge to sense perception. Just as Plato is often classified as a Rationalist, but he really isn't, by modern standards, so Aristotle, whom I classified as a modified Platonist, is often classified as an Empiricist, but he really isn't, by modern standards. For Aristotle says that even though all of our knowledge begins with sense experience, it does not end there; it leads to the Forms, by abstraction. All modern Empiricists speak strongly against abstraction and "abstract ideas." Empiricism reduces Aristotle as Rationalism reduces Plato.

The third modern epistemology is Kantianism. It's usually classified as Idealism, because it maintains that our ideas determine and form reality. Kant insists that he is *not* an Idealist, but he means by Idealism the teaching that ideas are the only reality, that what seems to be matter is really only mind or ideas. That is *metaphysical* idealism. Kant is an *epistemological* Idealist.

Kant tried to combine the two kinds of knowing that both Rationalism and Empiricism separated, but he did it not in the way Aristotle did, by abstracting the real Form from the real matter, nor in the way Plato did, by rising from the matter to the Form, but Kant combined the form and the matter by saying that we unconsciously *impose* the forms on the matter. For Kant the forms are only subjective and mental rather than objectively real, so that all the order we experience comes from our minds, not from objective reality. The ordered world as we know it is a product of unconscious human projection of innate universal forms *of thought* onto the unknowable formless material world out there. He calls this idea his "Copernican Revolution in philosophy."

These forms included three kinds, for Kant: first, the forms of external sense perception, time and space; second, logical categories like causality, necessity, or relation, and third the three basic "ideas of pure reason," as he called them, namely God, self, and world. None of these can be known to be objectively real, according to Kant. We cannot know objective reality, or what he calls "things in themselves," only how it appears to our minds after we have processed it through these three kinds of forms. Plato's Forms are objective; Kant's are subjective, though they're not different for different individuals. They're universal and necessary but subjective.

When we write the phrase "Plato's Ideas," always capitalize the word "Ideas," to distinguish it from concepts. Kant basically DEcapitalizes Plato's Ideas—or decapitates them, because for Plato their heads are in the heavens, but for Kant they're only in us.

(4) In listing the forms of modern Positivism or Reductionism I began with methodology and epistemology, because that's where modern philosophy begins, rather than with metaphysics. But if the most important part of philosophy is metaphysics, as it was for Plato, the most important reductionism is metaphysical reductionism. And the most common, most obvious, most simple, and most radical form of this is materialism, reducing all reality to matter, denying both *subjective* spirit, or mind, *and* objective spirit, or *Logos*, Platonic Ideas.

Materialism was a small minority view in ancient times, and simply nonexistent for over one thousand years in the Middle Ages, but increasingly popular in modern philosophy, beginning with Thomas Hobbes in the seventeenth century, and becoming more popular with the "philosophes" of the French Revolution in the eighteenth century, and becoming an ideological dogma for Marx, and for half the world for much of the twentieth century, between 1917 and 1989, the rise and fall of Communism. Materialism is still the working philosophy of the vast majority of popular writers of science in the world.

Materialism is the most obvious form of reductionism. It says simply that there *is* no world outside the cave of matter, and that we prisoners inside the cave are really only intelligent living rocks, parts of the cave. Man is that part of the universe that has somehow achieved such a degree of material complexity through the blind accident of natural selection that it can know the cave itself—the part can know the whole, the lesser can know the greater.

Materialism can't explain the difference between good and evil, the difference between Mother Teresa and Hitler. That difference can't be reduced to brain chemistry because the difference between love and hate is not the same *kind* of thing as the difference between the presence and absence of serotonin. If you disagree with that, you may know a lot about serotonin but you don't know much about love. If you think you can get qualities like moral goodness out of mere chemical quantities, you probably think you can get blood out of a stone, or a man out of a machine.

(5) And this brings us to anthropological reductionism, our fifth Positivism: reducing human knowers to something not qualitatively different from the universe we know. For the materialist, Man is essentially a machine. La Mettrie, in the seventeenth century, wrote a book with exactly that title, *Man a Machine*. B. F. Skinner, in the twentieth century, gave a more sophisticated version of that with his Behaviorism. Most thinkers don't quite go so far as to reduce man to a machine, but they do reduce man to a clever animal, and reduce human reason to the operation of the computer-brain and the rationalization of animal desire. Freud, for instance, says, on the last page of his most philosophical book, *Civilization and Its Discontents*, that the only thing he is certain of is that all reasoning is rationalizing, caused not by reason's insight into objective reality but by the strength of the desires of the libido or the id, and the demand to justify desire by a façade of reasons.

Of course, that form of skepticism, like all forms of skepticism, is self-contradictory, for it if *is* true, it is *not* true, because if it is true, then there is no such thing as the knowledge of objective truth, only the rationalizing of subjective desire; and if there is no such thing as the knowledge of objective truth, then that idea— that there is no such thing as the knowledge of objective truth— is also not knowledge of objective truth. If all reasoning is nothing but the rationalizing of desire, then the idea that all reasoning is nothing but the rationalizing of desire is also nothing but rationalizing of desires. "Nothing-but" is always self-contradictory. Nothing-buttery always melts itself away.

One of the most important aspects or subdivisions of anthropological reductionism is sexual reductionism, which began with Freud. Not only does he reduce almost everything to sex, but he reduces sex to something subhuman and impersonal. Since man is nothing but animal, love is nothing but lust, lust is nothing but sex, sex is nothing but orgasm, orgasm is nothing but chemistry. In fact for Freud everything, including art and science and religion and philosophy—and one would have to say, logically, Freud's own psychology too—is nothing but a substitute for sex. When the artist loves and paints the beauty of a sunset, it's a substitute for orgasm with the sun, since the sun is a bit too big and hot and far away for direct fulfillment of this desire. Freud calls even the affection of a mother for her infant "aim-inhibited affection," and says that all affection is originally sexual. If Freud actually ever said "sometimes a cigar is just a cigar," it's probably only because he was in love with the words "just," and "only," and "nothing but."

(6) The most practical, most life-changing division of philosophy is ethics, so the most important Positivistic reductionism is in ethics. For Plato, ethics goes all the way up, so to speak, into ultimate reality, because the ultimate reality is The Good, Values are the highest kinds of facts. There is no absolute fact-value distinction. Ethics is the knowing and living of ultimate Reality. It's not just obeying laws or satisfying conscience or doing your duty or helping others, it's also becoming more real, more like ultimate reality, which is Absolute Goodness.

The two main ethical options in modern philosophy, which you will always find in modern textbooks, are Utilitarian ethics and Kantian ethics. Utilitarian ethics is essentially pragmatism, being practical, getting results, doing whatever produces the most happiness in the most people. That's the only absolute; everything else is relative to that. Kantian ethics opposes that and says there is one ethical absolute, or, as he calls it, the "categorical imperative," which is essentially the Golden Rule, do unto others whatever you will that they do unto you and to everyone else. But it's a "whatever," it has no content, like the Ten Commandments, for instance. And it's not teleological; it's not for any other end, even happiness or human fulfillment.

Kantian ethics is called "deontological" ethics because it denies any ontology, any metaphysics, any claim to know objective reality, including the reality of human nature and its needs and its end and perfection and fulfillment, and therefore any law of its nature, any natural laws, as in a natural law ethic. Teleology, or purpose, is in modern times reduced to something subjective, so Utilitarian ethics is called teleological ethics, even though it too, like Kant, has no metaphysics, no objective end. It seeks only happiness, which is for typically modern minds always something subjective, not objective. "Happiness" in premodern ethics always meant objective perfection, because it assumed a Platonic Form of perfection, the perfection of human nature; but in modern times the word came to mean mere subjective satisfaction, because modern philosophers don't believe in the Platonic Form of perfect humanity. So Kant can't base an ethic on that kind of happiness; he has to base it on duty, and to sharply contrast duty to happiness and say that happiness has nothing to do with ethics, because happiness has become merely subjective, just as it has in Utilitarianism.

So the two main options in modern ethics both stem from the rejection of Platonism.

(7) And so do the two main options in modern *political* philosophy—our seventh Positivism. These two options are collectivism, as in Marx, and individualism, as in John Stuart Mill's Utilitarianism, according to which there *is* no common *good* by nature, only by convention and agreement, because there is no universal human *nature*. Man is not by nature a political animal in most modern political philosophers. And the reason for that is ultimately metaphysics.

Modern political philosophy, like modern ethical philosophy, is skeptical of metaphysics, and thus devoid of metaphysical content. The one metaphysical idea common to all premodern political philosophers except the Sophists was some notion of the natural end or goal or good of man socially and collectively, and political systems were based on this vision of the natural good for man. Nearly all influential modern political philosophers reject this and adopt the Social Contract Theory, which says that social good is artificial, the result of a contract, or positive law rather than natural law. In other words, modernity has regressed back to the Sophists. This is true not only of cynics like Machiavelli and pessimists like Hobbes but also optimists like Rousseau and idealists like Kant and Utopians like Marx. Modern political philosophy has lost faith and hope in knowing the objective essential nature of anything and therefore of the essence and end of man, and therefore of human society.

Montesquieu, in *The Spirit of the Laws*, pits ancient political philosophy, based on the good, or virtue, against modern political philosophy, based on freedom—the freedom to invent and work for any good you want as long as you don't get in the way of other people doing the same thing—and the modern option wins. John Stuart Mill in the nineteenth century and John Rawls in the twentieth century were the most prominent proponents of this metaphysically content-less politics. It's a consequence of Kant's position that we simply cannot know things in themselves, that we can't know real essences, and therefore we can't know the essence of man, and therefore we can't know the essential, natural end and purpose and destiny of man, and therefore we can't know the universal good of man, and therefore we can't know the good of human society. So it becomes simply a "whatever," whatever system works best to make most people happy, whatever keeps us free from what we all hate: poverty and death and war and violence. Freedom, not goodness, is the only thing we can agree on.

This is political Positivism as opposed to a natural law politics. The only influential force in the world that teaches a natural law politics any more is the Catholic Church, in the many social encyclicals from all the popes of the last one hundred fifty years. Even Islam, which has an elaborate, long social tradition, does not base it on philosophy or reason but sheer faith and obedience. Shari'a law is not a natural law but a positive law, posited by God rather than man.

(8) Another Positivism in modern philosophy is Logical Positivism. The term was used for a school of thinkers that began with

the so-called Vienna Circle in the early twentieth century and which dominated English speaking philosophy for a long time. Its bible was *Language, Truth, and Logic* by A. J. Ayer. Its bottom line conclusion was that all of traditional philosophy— philosophical theology, metaphysics, ethics, aesthetics, and philosophical anthropology— were literally meaningless (as Hume implied in that great rhetorical flourish at the end of his *Enquiry*: burn all the books of religion and metaphysics because only physical science and mathematics have any meaning). They are meaningless because they violated the Verification Principle, which states, first, that if a proposition cannot be verified, or proved, it is meaningless, and second, that the only two ways of verification are empirical observation or formal logical self-evidence. So every statement that is neither empirically verifiable nor a tautology is literally meaningless.

The majority of philosophers today who call themselves "analytic philosophers" and who concentrate on logical and linguistic analysis, as the Logical Positivists did, no longer hold that extreme view. In fact they explore many questions in metaphysics, ethics, and theology very fruitfully. The reason the movement died was that it is obviously self-eliminating, self-contradictory, because the Verification Principle—taken as a principle, a truth about propositions rather than merely an optional, practical method—contradicts itself. It says that all propositions that are not either tautologies or empirically verifiable are meaningless. But it itself is neither a tautology nor empirically verifiable. Therefore it is meaningless. So this philosophy was later modified from a "this is the way it is" manifesto to a "let's agree to do philosophy this way" practical method—something like the scientific method aimed at propositions instead of things. And that can be very useful, like narrow, concentrated laser light. But it cannot exclude or invalidate ordinary light. In fact, all methods of improved lighting (thinking) must begin with and presuppose ordinary light (thought).

(9) Our ninth Positivism is linguistic Positivism. Deconstructionism is the most radical form of linguistic Positivism. The

essential claim of Deconstructionism, as far as I can tell—I keep asking people who say they are Deconstructionists whether they make this claim, because I can't believe they do, but they all say they really do—the essential claim is that words do not have *intentionality*: they are not signs of things, and they do not get their truth or even their meaning from real things in the world.

According to premodern thought, since there is something like Platonic Ideas, things reflect these Ideas, so that *things* are also *signs*, *logoi*, words. We can look along them as well as at them; we can inquire about their *sign*ificance. This enquiry is unending and provokes our wonder. According to the modern mind, things are just things, not signs, because there are no Platonic Forms for them to signify. The last step in this reductionism is Deconstructionism. According to Deconstructionism, even words are not words, not signs, they are only things. Archibald MacLeish expressed this nicely in "Ars Poetica" when he said of poetry, "A poem should be palpable and mute / As a globed fruit. . . . A poem should not mean, / But be."

What meaning is there in life then? What is left? According to Deconstructionism, one thing is left: power. Because words are not signs of truth but only human acts designed to change other minds, they are expressions of the will to power rather than the will to truth. In other words Deconstructionism is Nietzsche applied to language. Words are not labels on things or pictures of things but little dynamite sticks in minds, and whoever is clever knows how to light the fuses. Since there is no truth, no *Logos*, nothing is really true or false, right or wrong, good or bad.

I must confess I find this the single most worthless, cynical, negative, and destructive idea I have ever discovered in the entire history of human thought. For it undermines absolutely everything. Nothing really means anything, including that sentence. Everything is reduced to a game of power. Do I jerk your brain's chain or do you jerk mine? Thrasymachus would have loved it. It's the philosophy of Big Brother in *1984*. And that's the *best* thing I can say about it.

We appreciate an idea best by looking at its most complete denial. It's like appreciating a friend best after he dies. We can thank Deconstructionism for helping us to appreciate Platonism by its most complete theoretical denial, at least in the sphere of language. In our next lecture, we will learn the same lesson, the importance of Platonism, by looking at the most complete practical and ethical and human and existential denials of it in various forms of Nihilism. We might call Nihilism the tenth and most deadly form of Positivism, because it nihilates, or denies, all real, objective value and meaning and purpose in human life. We might call this existential Positivism, and we need a whole other lecture to explore it.

Lecture VII:
Nihilism

Nihilism literally means the ism or ideology of nothing, or nothingness. It does not mean that nothing *exists*, of course; that would be self-contradictory, because in order to say that nothing exists, the speaker has to exist. Nihilism means that nothing has intrinsic *value*, or meaning, or purpose. As Sartre defines his existentialism, it means that nothing that has human *existence* has *essence*. There is no Platonic Form, no *Logos*.

Nihilism is a negative answer to the most fundamental question in practical or existential philosophy, in one's life-view, or *Lebensschauung*, as the Germans say, rather than in theoretical philosophy or world-view, or *Weltanschauung*. But this life-view has *roots* in a theory, a world-view, a metaphysics, as any ethical or practical philosophy always has.

Nihilism is the practical conclusion of a denial of Platonism in the basic sense we have defined it in these lectures, the denial of the existence of any transcendent *Logos*, any objective and universal good or end or teleology or purpose or value. It is the denial of all Platonic Ideas, but especially Plato's Big Idea, the Idea of the Good. For Nihilism, if there is any meaning and value to human life at all, it is arbitrary: we make it up ourselves as an artifice, a kind of game. Life really is what Macbeth called it, "a tale told by an idiot, full of sound and fury, signifying nothing." It has no significance, as in Deconstructionism, for it contains only things, not signs; things are not signs. There *are* no signs, no omens, no revelation, no message in the bottle from outside our little island, no light from a world outside our cave. Nihilism is the existential consequence of *Logos*lessness.

To see the difference Nihilism makes, compare Shakespeare's *Macbeth* with Faulkner's classic novel *The Sound and the Fury*. The latter takes its title from Macbeth's famous "Tomorrow and to-morrow and tomorrow" speech, when he is going morally insane with despair and damnation because he and Lady Macbeth have succumbed to the temptations and deceptions of the three witches, who are from hell, not from feminist consciousness-rais-ing circle dances. Macbeth has committed murder out of pure selfish ambition, and now he confesses that this is how life ap-pears now to him, "full of sound and fury, *signifying nothing*". That's Nihilism, exactly: no significance, no signifying, no word, no message, no *Logos*.

But Shakespeare frames this speech, and judges it, by his own medieval Christian worldview, so that the play becomes a cau-tionary tale, a warning about damnation. The frame interprets the picture. Shakespeare's worldview is that of the Middle Ages, which is the synthesis of Athens and Jerusalem, it is both Platonic and Judeo-Christian, both rational-moral and religious; and from this point of view Macbeth's life has great significance: the same significance as the life of Faust or of Judas Iscariot. It's called damnation: a very significant evil. But from Macbeth's point of view, life has *no* significance. And what Faulkner does in *The Sound and the Fury* is that he tells his story from Macbeth's point of view, not Shakespeare's or Plato's or Christ's. He shows us what life looks like when it is *in fact* only full of the sound and the fury but not the signifying.

Samuel Beckett did the same thing in *Waiting for Godot*, with a lot more hilarious, Monty Python-like humor. But the only rea-son many of us laugh at that play is because we still believe in and live in Shakespeare's world of meaning, not Beckett's world of Nihilism. *We* are not Vladimir or Estragon, we are not inside the play but outside it, as we are outside of *Macbeth* . The more totally and surely we live in the Platonic and Christian world, the more totally we break up with laughter at this play. But to the ex-tent that we live in the world of Nihilism, we are disturbed by it, and by its meaninglessness, and we can only pity but not laugh, because laughter means that there is a distance between you and what you laugh at. Fear is like laughter that way: it involves distance. That was what Shakespeare did: he evoked in his Christian audience the fear of Macbeth, fear of damnation. A saint would also *pity* Macbeth, as well as fear him, and a saint would pity Vladamir and Estragon as well as laugh at them, and the saint would have the most complete reaction, because that would be the most like God. (The fact that I laugh at Vladamir and Estragon rather than pitying them tells me that I am not a saint.)

Compare what Faulkner did with the Macbeth story with what Goethe did with the Faust story. Goethe also changed the frame, the point of view. In *Faust*, Goethe told the traditional moral story of Faust, the man who sold his soul to the Devil, from an antitraditional, antimoral point of view. Traditionally, the story of Faust was like the story of Macbeth: a cautionary tale about damnation, a moral and religious lesson. Its significance, its point, was the point of the most practical sentence ever uttered, by the most practical man who ever lived; "What does it profit a man to gain the whole world and lose his own soul?" But Goethe changed that 180 degrees. He went even farther away from the original story than Faulkner did: he sided with the devil, or the devil in Faust; Faust incorporates his own devil as well as his God, Faust accepts evil as well as good, he is told that he must become "better *and more evil*," and the true God turns out to be not the Judeo-Christian God but something like "the Force" in *Star Wars*: half evil and half good. Remember, the Force has a dark side. In *Faust* God and the Devil turn out to be allies, because they both move Faust up the ladder of enlightenment and maturity and away from his earlier moralistic innocence. It's very much like Nietzsche's "beyond good and evil." So the whole point and end of the old Faust story is turned into its opposite. Faust is not damned at all but enlightened. He is not punished but rewarded for disobeying the moral law.

So where Shakespeare showed us a Nihilist's mind and world from the perspective of a moralist, and where Faulkner showed us a Nihilist's mind and world from the perspective of a nihilist, Goethe showed us the world where heaven and hell, God and the devil, good and evil, are ultimately one, and that seems to me to be the most Nihilistic world of all because there is no ultimate choice, as in Shakespeare and no ultimate tragedy of meaninglessness, as in Faulkner and Beckett, and therefore no ultimate drama in life. Even though *Faust* is a great drama literarily, ultimately there *is* no drama in life if Goethe's worldview is true because there is no real difference between heaven and hell, good and evil. Instead there is what William Blake called "The marriage of heaven and hell," rather then what C.S. Lewis called "the great divorce." Only cultures that have believed in the great choice between some kind of heaven and hell have produced great drama. That's why the classical and Judeo-Christian West has produced so much greater drama than the East: because there is no eternal, ultimate Hell in the Eastern world view. *Ultimately*, all is one, all is Heaven, all is Brahman, or Buddha-mind, or Tao.

We've looked at Nihilism in four masters of drama and fiction (Shakespeare, Faulkner, Beckett, and Goethe). I'd like to survey twelve more philosophical thinkers, all eminently readable, who deal with Nihilism: the author of Ecclesiastes, who first wrote of it; Augustine, who lived through it; Pascal, the first modern thinker who diagnosed it; Kierkegaard, who overcame it by a leap of faith alone; Nietzsche, who went insane trying in vain to overcome it; Dostoyevsky, whose characters live it with passion; Tolstoy, who almost committed suicide because of it; Heidegger, one of the profoundest of modern philosophers who was haunted by Nietzsche; Camus, the most honest atheist novelist, who hated Nihilism but couldn't overcome it; Sartre, who thoroughly embraced Nihilism more clearly and totally than anyone else; and Marcel and Buber, Sartre's most trenchant critics, who offer a philosophy of Personalism as a modern way of escaping this modern disease. All of them are haunted by the death of Platonism, which is fundamentally what Nietzsche meant by the death of God.

Obviously I can only give you a salesman's sample of these great thinkers in one lecture, and that's precisely my purpose: to sell them, to send you to read them, because they are eminently readable and they all help to diagnose the fundamental disease at the heart of our civilization.

All of these philosophers can be called Existentialists, even though Heidegger, Marcel, and Buber all explicitly repudiated that label in order not to be confused with Sartre, who invented it. But Existentialism is much broader than Sartre. Existentialism is not a set of answers but a set of questions. There are atheistic and theistic, optimistic and pessimistic, nihilistic and anti-nihilistic Existentialists, but they all ask the same question about human existence: is it vanity of vanities, as the father of Nihilism, the writer of Ecclesiastes, called it?

Existentialists are not interested in abstract, theoretical questions, but only in practical, concrete questions, questions that make a difference to human existence. (They use the word "existence," by the way, to mean only *human* existence, not the existence of the universe or atoms or bugs or rocks.) Frankly, I find the existentialists the only modern philosophers that are really interesting, for that very reason: they ask the most interesting question, not the questions absent-minded professors ask. I can't help agreeing with William James's criterion of meaning (he mistakenly calls it a criterion of *truth*). He says truth is that which makes some real difference to my experience. He calls these truths, or questions about these issues "live issues," live questions as distinct from dead ones. Examples are the existence or nonexistence of God, free will, life after death, moral duty, and an objectively real, universal end and purpose and meaning to human life. Whether these five things are affirmed or denied makes a difference to one's life. In fact, they probably make the greatest difference. They make a difference to *everything* in your life. For instance, take life after death. Whether there is hope of life after death or not, of course you have to put one foot after the other on the way to death, but it makes a difference to each step whether you think the road ends in nothingness or in heaven. You can't choose to send your body away from that road to the grave, but you *can* choose to send your soul away in hope. *Or* you can believe you are reading Dante's sign over hell: "Abandon all hope, ye who enter here." You can choose. Not all existentialists *affirm* life after death, or the soul, or God, or morality, or ultimate meaning, but all of them affirm free choice.

The author of the book of Ecclesiastes is the first deliberate nihilist, the first metaphysical anti-Platonist, in history. His main point, "All is vanity," is the formula for *Logos*lessness. Ecclesiastes sees vanity everywhere. "Vanity" here means the inability to attain our end, purpose, or final cause, which is happiness and peace, success not just in business or sex or politics but in life. The author claims to be Solomon, the wisest and richest and most powerful man in Israel's history, but even though he got straight A's in all his subjects, he's flunking Life. His formula for unhappiness is simple: "What profit has man for all his toils under the sun?" In other words, it's Mick Jagger's simple and profound complaint: "You can't always get what you want" and "I can't get no satisfaction." The good we seek is not the good we find. All life is "toil," work, effort, attempt, hope; and the object of hope always eludes us.

The literal meaning of the Hebrew word for "vanity" is "a striving after wind." What good is it all? Remember that for Plato the Idea of the Good, Perfect Goodness, is the ultimate reality; and this for a Biblical Jew is God; and this is the only book in the Bible where God remains a silent object rather than a speaking subject. Emptiness reigns in His place—until the last few verses, probably written by a second author to answer the first author: "Here is the conclusion of the matter: fear God and keep His commandments, for this is the whole duty of man. For God will bring every work into judgment, whether good or evil." Judgment, justice, rightness—that was for Plato the key virtue that held everything else together. If that is missing in life, as the first author of Ecclesiastes claims, then life has no moral order, no moral meaning. It is a tale told by an idiot, full of sound and fury, signifying nothing.

The book of Ecclesiastes was probably included in the canon of scripture by the rabbis because it is a powerful apologetic for

God: it shows what life is like without Him. It is a reduction *ad absurdum*, a reduction to absurdity argument: if no God, no meaning. Nihilism can send us running to the rabbis. It is as up to date as Jean Paul Sartre, about two thousand five hundred years later.

Equally contemporary is Augustine's *Confessions*, an incomparably dramatic, poetic, thoughtful, and passionate story of Augustine's escape from a very modern kind of Nihilism: skepticism, and hedonism. It was written 16 centuries ago, but no living person who can read should be allowed to die without having read it. Please find Frank Sheed's translation of (Hackett Publ.) it; he's the only one who makes the English sing almost as beautifully and passionately as Augustine's Latin.

After rejecting the Manichean philosophy he had believed or a decade, Augustine became as existential skeptic and nihilist for a while. But his most fundamental struggle was with himself. He tried everything: all the available candidates for the high office of president of your life, road to happiness, peace, and joy, *summum bonum*, greatest good, or meaning of life. And he shows us how they all fail existentially as well as rationally. Everything else that seems to be something turns out to be nothing, as it did with Ecclesiastes. God is his last resort, and he wrestles and doubts and rebels and questions and runs away from the Hound of Heaven in every way he can, but eventually, by divine grace, he loses the wrestling match—and that's how he wins.

It's ridiculous enough to try to summarize 16 great books in 8 pages, but when one of them is Augustine's *Confessions*, the attempt is so absurd that even the attempt simply cannot happen. Beyond what I just said about the central theme, I can summarize this incredible, life-changing book only by three words: read it yourself.

Let's fast forward through the Middle Ages, the only age in which Nihilism is totally absent, to the beginning of modern times, when the dark sun of Nihilism begins to rise over many horizons. Go to Pascal, the great contemporary, critic and alternative to Descartes, the philosopher of Rationalism and optimism and humanism and the Enlightenment. Pascal was not a Nihilist but he understood Nihilism because he saw it rising in his day, the dawn of modernity, the late scientific Renaissance. Pascal lived in the mid-seventeenth century, but he sounds like he is alive today and watching us, especially when he speaks of three things that permeate our lives and show our Nihilism: generalized boredom, diversion, and indifference. When my students read these sections of Pascal, they always get suddenly quiet. They thought they were safely looking into a book and they suddenly saw the face of Pascal looking at *them* from its pages.

In his *Pensées* he argues that Christianity alone can explain the four primary pieces of existential data about universal humanity: we all seek certainty; we all find ignorance and doubt instead; we all seek happiness; and we all find wretchedness instead. Worse, to cover up our failure, we invent lies. The new lie of our age, which Pascal exposed, was that science can explain everything and technology will make us happy. Pascal, by the way, was one of the greatest scientists of all time. Among other things he invented the world's first working computer. That's why a computes language is named after him.

A symptom of our unhappiness is boredom. It is a uniquely modern phenomenon; a distinct word for general boredom simply does not exist in any premodern language. War and pain and death do not drive a man crazy; meaninglessness does. Nietzsche said, two centuries later, that a man can endure almost any *how* if only he has a *why*. Lacking a *why*, an end, a *Logos*, a reason to live and a reason to die, man can no longer endure even mild inconvenience and discomfort, and demands a technological solution to every problem. That's us. Pascal says we can find the source of all our misery, and the wars we fight to fill the emptiness, in the fact that we can't stand to be totally alone with ourselves in our own room for one hour. We need diversion to divert ourselves from ourselves.

Even stupider than diversion is indifference to the very questions of whether there is meaning and purpose to life and death, whether there is anything like God and the Good. We do not dare to care. We turn our souls into wet spaghetti noodles, and our lives into "entertainment." We give up hope, we obey Dante's sign over the entrance to Hell. But if there *is* no ultimate Good to attain, we cannot hope to attain it. Without this fundamental metaphysical Platonism, life itself becomes not worth living.

For an incisive diagnosis of the modern heart, and for clues to an exit from this cave, read Pascal's *Pensées*.

Two centuries after Pascal, Kierkegaard offered an equally stunning psychological diagnosis and religious cure for Nihilism, especially in *Either/Or* and *The Sickness Unto Death*. His diagnosis of Nihilism was psychologically brilliant, but the cure was a pure "leap of faith" not based on reason. For Kierkegaard, a Lutheran, was a Nominalist like Luther, and distrusted reason. He called the central doctrine of Christianity, the Incarnation, "the absolute paradox," and gave no reason for embracing it rather than a hundred other options. Pascal at least gave us a practical reason, the famous "wager," and many theoretical reasons that he deemed at least probable, such as saints, miracles, prophecies, and Jewish history.

Nietzsche and Kierkegaard are often called the two founders of Existentialism, yet no two philosophers were ever more totally opposed. Kierkegaard said that everything he ever wrote—a stunning variety of books from many different perspectives or points of view, not all of them religious—constituted a carefully planned missionary plot; that it was all about only one thing, the process by which a concrete individual could "become a Christian." Nietzsche, on the other hand, called himself "the Antichrist" and Christianity his number one target. Both concentrated on the lonely, alienated individual in a world without objective reason, the post-Platonic world of *Logos*lessness, a world where reason said that God is dead. So all they had left was the leap of faith, and both took the leap, but in opposite directions. Nietzsche's only argument for his atheism was a deliberately, provocatively personal one: "I will now disprove the existence of all gods. If there were gods, how could I bear not to be a god? *Consequently*, there are no gods." That is Irrationalism with a vengeance.

But the consequences of this leap are worked out with ruthlessly rational consistency, although Nietzsche's writing style is anything but rational—he seems perpetually overheated, like a car without antifreeze, or a bomb about to explode. When he proclaimed that "God is dead," he meant all gods, all transcendence, all vestiges of the Platonic world outside the cave, including objective truth and objective values. Science, democracy, human rights, justice, reason, metaphysics, humanism, values like love, justice, mercy, rational self-control, tenderness, compassion—all these values are now undermined, devalued.

Nietzsche thought of himself as a prophet of the new man, the "overman" or "Superman," who is not a man but a next *species*. Having killed God, he has also killer God's image in man, moral conscience. Like Dostoyevski, Nietzsche believed that "if God does not exist, everything is permitted." He would not have been surprised by the fact that into the nihilistic gap a monster like Hitler could easily step. Remember that haunting scene from the movie *Cabaret* where the passionate, fanatical, goose-stepping Nazi youth march into the bored, decadent outdoor café singing "tomorrow belongs to me"? Nietzsche would have despised Hitler's politicism, nationalism, and racism, but he would not have been shocked by his cruelty or his lies. Nietzsche's new god, the Overman, is the creator of new values and even of truth itself. Nietzsche was the first philosopher in history to seriously ask the question he called "the most dangerous question," the question "why truth?" He questioned the universal will to truth, exalting will over mind absolutely and glorying in its arbitrariness. He wrote, "Why not rather untruth?" It is a disconcertingly difficult question to answer without begging the question by saying "well, the true answer to that question, the true reason for truth, is. . . . " At the very least, Nietzsche brilliantly and daringly showed that truth is either an absolute unjustifiable by anything more absolute, or not an absolute at all but an option, a choice of the will. And that is the most radical departure from the Platonic tradition in the history of human thought.

Tolstoy, perhaps the world's most perfect novelist, addresses the question of Nihilism not merely in his characters but above all in himself, in his autobiography, *Confession*. We are shocked to read that after becoming the most famous and beloved writer in the world after publishing *War and Peace*, with all his honors and glory and money and estates and a loving family, he confessed that for many years he saw no answer to the problem of life's meaning, and that his first thought upon waking up each morning was, "I hope I will not commit suicide today." Only when he listened to the simple peasants instead of to his educated, intellectual friends, did he find any meaning and any hope, and it was in their simple, blind faith and innocent love alone. Tolstoy's *Confession* is a book that the Pulitzer Prize-winning writer Robert Coles repeatedly used with stunning success in his courses at Harvard, where all his students identify with intellectuals like Tolstoy, and not with the peasants and their simple faith. Unfortunately, Tolstoy himself never reconciled his faith and his reason, and lived with constant unresolved tensions and contradictions between the two in his own mind. But at least he lived; he chose life, even if he could not explain or justify the choice.

Dostoyevsky, the profoundest of novelists, gives us two great characters who incarnate Nietzsche's Overman, in perhaps the two greatest novels ever written, Ivan Karamazov in *The Brothers Karamazov*, and Raskolnikov in *Crime and Punishment*. Both of them, like Nietzsche, end up literally insane. Nietzsche and Dostoyevsky were not thrill-seeking decadents or teenage rebels fascinated with insanity and darkness and rebellion and evil for their own sake; they were prophets, and Western civilization has not yet heeded their warnings. Without *Logos*, without Platonic Ideas, without the Idea of the Good, without a metaphysical basis for living and choosing, without belief in an objective reality that is greater than the material walls of the cave and the subjective will of the cave dwellers, the only two possible human futures are either the Nietzschean insanity of absolute rebellion against all order or the bored quietude of what Nietzsche called "the last man," the clever ape addicted to creature comforts, full of what Pascal called diversions and indifference and what Huxley called *Brave New World*.

Martin Heidegger, unlike all the other names I'll talk about in this lecture, is notoriously difficult to read and understand, but he is the only major metaphysician of the twentieth century. He was haunted by Nietzsche, especially the consequences of the "death of God," and tried to think his way out of the modern Nihilism that Nietzsche so brilliantly portrayed, like a survivor digging out of the ruins and rubble of Berlin after the war. He did this by returning to the notion of Being, but in a deliberately anti-Platonic way. He blamed Plato for setting Western philosophy on a wrong road, the road of objectivity, and offered a mysterious but fascinating alternative notion of being, that sounds more like Zen Buddhism or Taoism than anything Western. If you want to tackle Heidegger I suggest reading three relatively short and easy things: (1) the first chapter of *An Introduction to Metaphysics*, called "the fundamental question", which is "why is there anything at all rather than nothing?"; (2) The introduction to his magnum opus "Being and Time;" and (3) the short almost Buddhist dialog *Discourse on Thinking*, about overcoming reason to reach Being.

I must warn you, though, that profound philosophers can be political idiots. Heidegger enthusiastically joined the Nazi party, called Hitler the new god, and even after the war never apologized for this. I explain this by that scene in *Cabaret*. In a nihilistic, *Logos*less world, even a perverse *Logos* can capture the mind. Nature abhors a vacuum spiritually as well as physically.

Albert Camus shows us Nihilism in practice in his novels, especially *The Stranger*, which shows us ourselves as Merseault, the antihero, the modern man who has no passion, for life or for death—either his recently deceased mother's, or his murder victim's, or his own. The only thing he ever becomes passionate against is the priest in his jail cell the day before his execution telling him he has an immortal soul and will go to either heaven or hell. That he cannot stand; his only passion is against religion because religion is the only validation for an absolute passion.

Camus shows us Nihilism not as rebellion (his nonfiction book *The Rebel* is actually almost a heroic book) but as tedium, boredom, emptiness. But in his haunting novel *The Plague* his atheist hero, Dr. Rieux, like Camus himself, has one passion and one meaning to life: he knows that "the meaning of life is to be a saint." So he heroically stays in African to help the helpless victims of the plague instead of going back to France and comfort. But he also knows that you can't be a saint without God, and he cannot believe in God. That was Camus's predicament all his short life. For a while he and Sartre were friends, but Sartre could not stand Camus's moral honesty and passion, so he repudiated his friendship with Camus.

Jean-Paul Sartre gives us perhaps the most perfect definition of Platonism in the history of philosophy, because he is the complete, perfect anti-Platonist, the perfect negative photo, the silhouette of Plato's absence.

Sartre invented the term "Existentialism" and defined it in such a way that it is the exact opposite of Platonism, both in its metaphysical core and in its anthropological and ethical consequences. Let's explore those two dimensions of Sartre's most radical alternative to Platonism.

It begins in his concept of being. Essentially, *there is no being*. That is the literal meaning of "Nihilism": nothingness. What could this possibly mean, *There is no being*? We can see it by contrasting it with Heidegger's metaphysics. Heidegger claims that traditional metaphysics was based on the mistake of confusing Being itself with a being, an object, a thing, a substance, or at best the mistake of approaching the meaning of Being itself through an exploration of the being of objects or substances, which Plato began and Aristotle developed. All Aristotle's logical categories apply to beings, but not to being itself, according to Heidegger. He proposed the alternative approach to being itself through an exploration of human be-ing, or human existing, which he called *Dasein*, being-there, and which he saw as a fundamentally different mode of being than the being of an object. Both objects and conscious subjects participate in being, but in fundamentally different ways. Man is not just the highest object, the rational animal; he is a different mode of being. If we begin with Heidegger, we can summarize Sartre as Heidegger minus Being. There is only what Sartre calls being-for-itself, which is the being of a subject (Heidegger's *Dasein*), and being-in-itself, which is the being of an object; and the two have nothing in common, no common Being to participate in.

Sartre also calls being-for-itself "existence" and being-in-itself "essence," and his point in separating these two is that nothing that exists—no human subject—has essence, or meaning, or *logos*, and no essence, no *Logos*, has existence. Subjects and objects have nothing in common because there is no Being itself that they both share. That's the essential metaphysical meaning of Nihilism: there is no Being. You might imagine a parallel this way: man and nature have something in common if there is a single God who designed and created both, but if you subtract God the Father, man and nature are no longer brother and sister. "Being" for Sartre functions like God; since for him there is no God, there is no Being.

Sartre says this atheism is the fundamental principle of his philosophy. He says: "Existentialism is nothing else than an attempt to draw all the consequences of a coherent atheist position." Sartre's first premise is atheism, or theological Nihilism, the nothingness of God; and here is its first consequence: it is metaphysical Nihilism, the nothingness of Being.

Sartre immediately draws a second consequence, a Nihilism in anthropology: "there is no human nature, since there is no God to conceive it. Man is nothing else than what he makes of himself."

This anthropological Nihilism follows from Sartre's meta-physical Nihilism. We have existence but no essence. Man exists, but has no meaning, no design, no *Logos*, since there is no God to design him. He designs himself, and nothing can justify him in designing one meaning or another.

And that is the basic consequence of Nihilism in ethics: no justification, no justice. There are no values except the ones I arbitrarily create. The only real value is my own freedom and autonomy. Values do not judge me; I judge values. I make a thing good or bad; I justify it by choosing it, rather than any objective good justifying my choice. I am in the place of God, and an arbitrary, tyrannical, irrational, fundamentalist God at that. There is nothing even remotely like Plato's Idea of the Good.

Sartre could summarize his ethics by changing just one word in the famous statement of moral relativism that Shakespeare puts into the mouth of Hamlet as he is pretending to be insane (a statement, by the way, that most moderns consider wise and enlightened, though Shakespeare considered it asinine): "There is nothing right or wrong but thinking makes it so," Sartre would say, "There is nothing right or wrong but willing makes it so."

The only absolute is the individual's freedom. Nietzsche made the will to power the end rather than a means, and Sartre does the same to freedom. He writes, "Freedom can have no other aim than to want itself; if man has once become aware that he imposes values, he can no longer want but one thing, and that is freedom." Therefore "one may choose *anything* if it is on the grounds of free involvement." Sartre himself chose to justify and glorify Marxist violence against the West, and Pol Pot studied Sartre's philosophy before murdering one-third of his people, including everyone who could read and write. It was a stunning verification of Dostoyevsky's prophecy that "if there is no God, everything is permissible."

Thus for Sartre's Nihilism there is no *Logos* either in being, or in man, or in life. Life is literally meaningless, absurd. This is the consequence of a fundamental anti-Platonism. We can be grateful to Sartre for articulating it so clearly and consistently. He is such a good evangelist for Nihilism that he functions as a counter spy; he sends sane readers screaming into the arms of Plato, or Christ.

Sartre's *Existentialism and Human Emotions* is a very short, clear, and readable summary of his philosophy in the abstract. And he also gave us a perfect fictional picture of his philosophy in the concrete in his brilliant little play *No Exit*. But I think Samuel Beckett, especially in *Waiting for Godot*, did an even better job of presenting Nihilism in concrete practice that is, in story form. Here is a play about nothing, or rather about nothingness. The plot is essentially that nothing happens for two acts; or, rather, nothingness happens. I find that students react to this play more variously than any other piece of literature I know. They divide into three groups. Some think it utterly stupid and silly. They are the ones who are so commonsensical that they can't even raise the question of *Logos* versus *Logos*lessness. A second group think it disturbingly profound and profoundly disturbing. These are the ones who are close to Nihilism themselves, or whose skeptical beliefs logically result in Nihilism, and the play shows them how utterly unhappy they are. A third group think it utterly hilarious. They are the Platonists, who know there is a world outside the cave and can laugh at as well as pity the prisoners who simply will not move from their misery.

Sartre's most trenchant critic was Gabriel Marcel, who point by point offered an alternative to Sartre. The best introduction I know to the two essentially different kinds of Existentialism, Sartre's nihilistic, atheistic, pessimistic version and Marcel's humanistic, theistic, and optimistic version, is the first two essays in Marcel's *The Philosophy of Existentialism*. One of them summarizes Sartre and the other one summarizes the seven basic themes in Marcel's own philosophy; and the very first theme is that there is Being, and that Being is the Good, or real intrinsic value. This is the heart of Platonism. Marcel, however, approaches this good not by rational argument but by a concrete phenomenological analysis of ordinary human experience. Intrinsic value is not a

116

metaphysical abstraction for Marcel, as it is for Plato, but is incarnated in every person. Marcel is a personalist. His other themes all follow this personal rather than abstract rational pattern, and include a defense of mysteries as distinct from problems, of self-knowledge, which he calls "recollection", of hope, creative fidelity, and "availability," or openness to other persons that is self-giving or charity and that Sartre declared impossible. In his second chapter Marcel very clearly and fairly explains Sartre's denial of these basic human values and devastatingly refutes it appealing to experience rather than abstract reason, as Plato did, to answer the immoralists and Sophists of his modern time.

I and Thou, by Rabbi Martin Buber, is a poetic version of Marcel's personalism. Like Marcel's work it retrieves *Logos*, real ultimate meaning and value, in a personal rather than a rational and argumentative way, through the encounter of an I with a Thou, a subject-subject rather than subject-object relationship.

Marcel and Buber are not household words; but the Personalist philosopher who *is* almost a household word, who is probably the most famous name among twentieth century philosophers, is Pope John Paul II. He is not easy to read, but he has created a revolution by joining the modern subjective and personalist approach with traditional objective values and natural law thinking as in Thomas Aquinas.

This more subjective and personal approach is not, I am convinced, an alternative to Plato's objective and rational one but complementary to it. And I believe this confluence, between objective metaphysics and the new Personalism, in its affirmative form à la Marcel and Buber rather than its negative, nihilistic form in Nietzsche and Sartre, is the philosophy of the future, and of the future of Western civilization. As we emerge from the cave and approach we discover two things: Being and ourselves, the "Am" and the "I" that are equally absolute aspects of the God of the burning bush, or, if you prefer safer philosophical abstractions, of ultimate reality.

Augustine, in his *Soliloquys*, imagines God asking him, "What do you want to know?" And he answers, "Only two things:

yourself and myself." I think that's wise; that's it; that's where it's at; that's the whole deal. For those are the only two realities that have eternal and intrinsic and absolute value, and also the only two realities that none of us will ever be able to ignore or escape either in time or in eternity. So we had better get to know them now, and it's not too late to begin. Isn't that, ultimately, the reason for studying philosophy? It was for Socrates.

I've painted a dark picture of Western civilization's departure from Platonic wisdom during modern times, through its three basic denials of Nominalism, Positivism, and Nihilism. But I look at the present philosophical decline not with hopelessness but with hope. I am convinced that the human heart is too big to be satisfied with the cave, however comfortable our technology makes it. Despite all our improvements in lifestyle, our lives are less satisfying than ever. We have far less pain, but far more discontent: more depression, more suicide. And this, to me, is a good sign! We are not content with our cave. It is our unhappiness, not our happiness, that gives me hope.

I see many signs of hope, not so much in philosophy but in the real world and in human nature. Whoever designed these two things, it was, thank God, not philosophers! In the concluding lecture I'd like to explore some real, not just philosophical, roads outside the cave, some chinks in the pitiless walls of the world, some fingerprints of transcendence. They are death, love, sex, the sacred, inspiration, art, nature, the heart, mystical experiences, and saints.

Lecture VIII:
Doors Out of Plato's Cave:
Signals of Transcendence in Our World

In this last lecture I want to look at some signals of transcendence, cracks in the cave walls, patches of light from outside the cave, which are not just for philosophers but for everyone in our post-Platonic world. We'll seem to go beyond Plato here, but throughout these lectures I have defined Platonism broadly, not just as the logical teaching that universals exist independently, but as the claim of metaphysical transcendence, that reality transcends the cave of ordinary human experience.

Let's begin with the most obvious and universal crack in the cave, death. Death looks like the end: a door into darkness; yet the vast majority of all human beings who have ever lived have believed that it is a new beginning, a door into light, not darkness; up, not down. This is even true today, even in our so-called secular society, especially when people actually approach that door. We then discover our natural instinct to believe, or at least to hope.

Platonism becomes very personal when we think about death. This is also true of the question of God. Death makes us ask not just "Is there a God?" but "Will I meet God?" And it is not argument but experience that will answer that question.

I use the word "God" here in a broad sense, as a real being superior to us and stronger than death. The two questions, Is there a God? and Is there life after death? are logically related; for only if there *is* something stronger than death can we hope to experience it after we die. So the practical payoff of Platonism, so to speak, is the hope for our own destiny beyond death. That hope strongly motivated even the agnostic Socrates. In his swan song in the *Apology*, he called this only a *hope* rather than a proof, although Plato later tried to prove it, both in the *Phaedo* and in the

Republic. Judge for yourself how good the proofs are; I find the strongest proof in the example of Socrates rather than in the arguments of Plato.

How can we know what happens at death? We know what happens to *bodies* at death. They do not go up but down. If they *are* resurrected in the end, as religious Jews, Christians, and Muslims believe, it can only be by a divine miracle, which is unprovable and unpredictable by mere philosophical reason, but only knowable by religious faith in a divinely revealed promise. But there are good arguments for the soul's immortality, if only we *have* souls; for whatever souls are made of, it's not mortal molecules. Bullets and cancer don't kill thoughts or loves, only organs. If we're more than apes plus computers, if we're *persons*, then we can hope to live after death. If there are no persons after death, there are no persons before death either, and we are confusing machines with persons. We are only cyborgs, cybernetic organisms, animal-based *machines*. But machines don't ask questions. Computers do only what you program them to do, they don't question their programming (unless you program them to do that). The most obvious signal of our transcendence of death is the fact that we raise that question, that we philosophize. Neither apes nor computers philosophize.

Even atheists like Freud admit that the belief in the spiritual soul and its immortality is innate, natural to us—though they think it is a natural illusion, like belief in God. Let's see what that psychological fact entails. The fact is that the vast majority of human beings have believed in both a God and a life after death. If they are wrong, then this vast majority have centered their lives on a fundamental and foundational illusion, and the only people who have been quite sane are the tiny elite minority of unbelievers, almost entirely concentrated in Western Europe and North America and in the last few centuries. I use the word "sane" deliberately. If all supernatural, immortal reality is an illusion, then nearly all of us are as insane as Jimmy Stewart in that old movie *Harvey*, who believes in an invisible giant rabbit that isn't there. God is just a bigger Harvey, And life after death and God almost always go together as a package deal. Atheists almost always deny both. My argument is simply that if they're right, we're almost all insane; that belief in the sanity of most of the human race is the price you have to pay for denying that death is a door out of the cave. That doesn't prove it is, but it shows you that you have to be a snob to be an atheist. That's probably why most atheists are reluctant to classify religion as insanity, as collective hallucination, as Freud quite frankly and logically does.

Death is the biggest door out of the cave, but there are also many little doors, and most of them are little deaths too: death of ordinary consciousness, as in mystical experiences; or death of the ego, as in the saints; or death of control, as in sexual orgasm or in artistic inspiration. There's a reason to believe that death may be the very best thing that happens to us, because all these other great things that happen to us are little deaths. They look like clues. In Plato's *Phaedo*, Socrates told his friends who were already mourning him before he died, "To fear death is to be unwise, because it is to think you know what you do not know: namely, that death is something bad. Who knows that death is not perhaps the very best thing?"

It is certainly a *hope* available to everyone, even in the absence of faith, and a faith available even in the absence of proof. But there is one absolute requirement: the prisoner must what to get out of the cave, and therefore must want there to *be* a greater world outside the cave, before he will make any effort to find the way to it. There are four steps: desire, hope, faith, proof. Most people don't get to the fourth step, as Plato did, or thought he did, but almost everyone at least gets to the first step. Without that, there's no hope of anything more. The heart must lead the head. Love and desire must come first. And that's quite Platonic. In the *Symposium*, Socrates says that he is willing to join the cycle of speechmaking about love, because, he says, "love is the only thing I claim to know about." Philosophy itself is a love, the love of wisdom.

A second clue is our own hearts. I think this is the single most irrefutable clue of all. Whatever else we mean by the heart—

feeling, intuition, willing, choosing—we always mean the power in us that loves, that longs, that desires. Platonism appeals to the heart as well as the head, longing as well as thinking, because it tells us that our hearts' deepest and most mysterious desire, the desire for a Good that is infinite and eternal and perfect, is a valid clue to truth, that it corresponds to reality. Thus the heart can lead the head.

We can raise this from a clue to an argument. Every *other* innate, natural, and universal desire of our hearts matches a reality; why not this? There is no natural hunger that has no real food. If we've learned to trust our hearts, as we learn to trust our mothers, because they've delivered on every promise they've made to us, why should we believe that this biggest promise of all is a cheat and a lie? It's trust, not proof, but the onus of proof is on the mistruster. We can't *prove* our mother is trustable, but we can't prove she isn't either, and all the evidence points to trust. How cynical to say it's all a dark plot, luring us with a million appetizers and then denying us the main course! What possible reason could you have for labeling mother that kind of a sadist? Wouldn't it be insane to believe *that* without proof?

When we compare Plato with Hobbes or Marx or Machiavelli or Sartre, we at least *hope* Plato is right, unless we are sadomasochists. We may *believe* he's not right, we may believe he made up all that stuff about a world of perfection outside the cave, but we don't *want* to believe that unless we are mad or insanely jealous of those who do believe it. Now this fact that we *want* to believe it, that we want to believe that Plato and all the religions of the world are right in this essential claim, this good news about there being more, more reality beyond matter, more goodness beyond imperfection, more life beyond death—the fact that it meets our hearts' deepest longing—why should that fact count *against* its truth rather than for it?

Let's look at our hearts a little more closely and focus on what we mean by love, since that's the heart's work. When Plato speaks of Love, especially in the *Phaedrus* and the *Symposium*, he means *Eros* (desire), not yet *Agape* (charity). A kind of *Agape* enters in

Plato too, but only *after* the prisoner has escaped from the cave. Then he has the charity to sacrifice the joys of the higher world to return to the cave to try to liberate the other prisoners. But the love that gets him out of the cave in the first place is *Eros*, desire.

Desire for what? Here's the problem. It's a desire for a "what" that we cannot confidently name as we can name all other objects of desire. It's not just a desire for more of the same. That would eventually be boring, like ten thousand years in Hawaii. It's a desire for something we've never possessed in this world, which is why we hope for another world. Our lover's quarrel with the world, our "divine discontent," our Augustinian "restless heart," is what Plato means by this *Eros*.

All *Eros* is for something beautiful, and there are many beautiful things in this world—spiritual beauties like justice and charity and physical beauties like a woman's face or a snow-covered forest; and we can have these, but we want something more: we want Beauty Itself, the thing all these different beauties come from and lead to. Even when all our other desires are satisfied, our heart still asks the mysterious question: "Is that all there is?" Our *Eros* is bigger than the sum total of its objects in this world. That is why there has to be more. Otherwise our *Eros* is meaningless. Or a dark plot to deceive us.

You can suppress that desire, but it's there to suppress. And it's the most significant desire of all, because if it's a cheat, all is lost. For this we would gladly exchange all the little toys we *can* get, all the little beauties we can contemplate in nature or human art, and all the little joys we can get from wine and women and song. (Never speak disparagingly of wine, women, or song, by the way, for God invented all three, according to the Bible.)

This desire is not a proof but it's a datum, and a clue, and we can look along it as well as at it, we can read it as a sign, like the hands of a clock or a compass needle. *Eros* is a compass; there must be a magnetic pole. *Eros* is an arrow: there must be a target. *Eros* is a hunger: there must be food, there must be the truth and goodness and beauty that we seek when we experience our little truths and goods and beauties and keep saying "Is that all there is?" We've tasted a million appetizers; there must be a main course.

Eros is our strongest road out of the cave. Plato is no cold Rationalist; philosophy for him is a love affair with Wisdom, the courtship of a goddess.

Eros is more than sex, but sex is a third door out of the world because it is a way of being out of your body and out of your mind. The sexual ecstasy, or standing-outside-yourself, that we do attain in this world points beyond itself, according to Plato in the *Symposium*. Sexual *Eros* seeks something impossible to attain in the world of time, something eternal; that's why it begets children, Plato says, futurity being a temporal substitute for eternity.

An orgasm is like a mystical experience. You lose control; you lose ordinary consciousness—and this is not a loss, but a gain, because it is a sign of what we are programmed for, destined for. It's an image of spiritual orgasm, an image of mystical experience, an earthly appetizer of heavenly food, a preview of the highest level of life outside the cave. We're programmed for that, that's why we long for that, that's why we're so addicted to it. We're programmed for ecstasy and we're satisfied with nothing less than ecstasy, standing-outside-yourself, outside ego-consciousness and egotism. Every religion in the world in some way acknowledges that mystical fact in demanding that we transcend our very self, displace our ego, get off the throne of our own lives. That's why Plato is the natural ally of all religions.

Sexual orgasm is also an image of the wonder that is the beginning of philosophy. As Josef Pieper writes, "just as in the erotic convulsion something happens that does not simply lie within man's free disposition, so the philosophical search for wisdom cannot be understood as an act set in motion exclusively by man. . . . Man must by virtue of his very nature ask questions that transcend his ability to comprehend. . . . man, as Pascal put it, transcends himself." In other words, even if we may control our answers we do not control our deepest questions. Although there may be a method for getting answers, there is no method for the wonder that prompts the questions. Wonder is like sex; it does not argue; it does not move its mouth in words; it just opens its mouth in an O and says "Oh!"

Sexual *Eros*, personal romantic love as distinct from merely animal passion, is not just a desire, it is also a vision. To *love* someone is to *see* them truly, as Dante saw Beatrice. Beauty is *not* in the eye of the beholder. Love is *not* blind. Love gives you eyes. We all know this, deep down. Whom do you trust to know you best: your uneducated friend who loves you truly, though he may be broken in many ways, or the world's greatest psychologist, who is brilliant and whole and happy but doesn't love you, but just uses you as a case study? The verdict is not in doubt.

So Dante is right: Beatrice really *is* a goddess (or at least an icon), and only the lover sees her truly. The religious corollary would be that that has to apply to God as well: the reason why God knows us totally is because he loves us totally.

A fourth door out of the cave is the sense of the sacred, which is the psychological origin of all the world's religions. The very existence of the category of the sacred testifies to something that cannot be explained in this-worldly categories.

The sense of the sacred does not mean something conventional like an ordained clergyperson but something natural like awe; not merely a humanly designated place like a church or time like a Sabbath, but something discovered, not invented. For instance the fear of a ghost, or a spirit, or a god, is a sacred fear, and that's a different *kind* of fear than any secular fear like the fear of a tiger, or a bullet, or a cancer. It is not a fear of what can be done to you—ghosts never harm you—but simply the fear of what it *is*: that is it something from outside our comfortable world, our cave.

This sense of the sacred is certainly diminishing in our modern world, for the obvious reason that our lives are filled with secular noise and man-made things that we *do* understand and control. But it still breaks through in those dangerous silences between the notes of our artificial musics. It breaks through also in madness, in demonic evil like the Holocaust, as well as in saints like Mother Teresa. We can't digest either of these two foods by purely secular stomachs; we can't break them down into something else, as we do with ordinary foods. They pass through us unchanged, like ghosts. Neither Mother Teresa nor Hitler can be explained by purely secular categories. There's something otherworldly about both of them, something that smells like it came from heaven or hell—if we still have that instinctive sense of spiritual smell.

A fifth signal of transcendence in ordinary life is what we call inspiration: the rising of some creative idea, like a bubble, to the surface of our consciousness. Where did it come from? Our unconscious mind? I don't think so, because that's what functions in sleep, but we're not wiser but *stupider* when we sleep. That sleeping mind, that unconscious mind, is what we lived by when we were one year old, but these creative ideas aren't the ideas of a toddler but of a genius. Even ordinary people sometimes just get these really great ideas now and then. I couldn't have written 70 books without them. When people ask me, I honestly don't know how I do it. Many writers will tell you that.

And these inspirations come not only to the mind but to the will too. A coward will suddenly become courageous, and rise to heroism, quite unpredictably. Sudden moral conversions happen, like sudden religious conversions. Why? Religion's answer is divine grace. Nobody can prove that, but that's what it looks like. It's at least a clue, a superhuman fingerprint on the weapon.

Sudden *joys* also happen, what Chesterton calls "joy without a cause." Nothing happens without a cause, so he really means joy without a natural cause, a human cause. Like total peace when the doctor tells you that you're going to die within a year. Joyful laughter suddenly erupting in the middle of tears. Of course you can explain it by brain chemistry if you want to—but why do you want to? You don't have to. You can read the clue, you can look along the crack in the cave wall and see a little of the world beyond, instead of just staring *at* it. You *can* explain a pointing finger by its muscle action. You can explain the spiritual end by the physical means. But that's like explaining a book by ink and paper. It's like eating a book instead of reading it. It's what a baby or an animal does. It's a denial of *Logos*.

Other signs, other words in the book of life are sudden rescues, sudden coincidences, things that look like divine providence—everyone has these stories to tell. Do you explain these stories by an explosion of ink in a print factory, or do you read the sign language of events and seek their significance? The word "significance" begins with the word "sign."

All the religions of the world accept that invitation to read the signs. The different religions all read somewhat different things in the book of life, but not *wholly* different things. And they all read the book instead of eating it. They look through the chinks in the walls of the world, they look along the road up and out of the cave instead of just at it. Or to use a Buddhist image for same Platonic point: a finger is useful for pointing to the moon, but the fool mistakes the finger for the moon.

There is a sixth door in the cave, or rather a whole series of doors, in *the arts*. Take music, the most mysterious and most powerful of the arts. Some music sounds in your heart different in kind, not just in degree, from all other music, as if it was echoing from the Garden of Eden before the Fall, like the faint echoes of radiation from the Big Bang that science still hears.

Some paintings and statues are more than just intriguing objects in the world; they are holes in the world, they invite us out of the world, like the wardrobe that drew the Pevensie children into Narnia—or, in a later book in the series, like the painting of the ship *The Dawn Treader* that the children stared at on the wall and that drew their bodies after their minds into itself, into the ship, into Narnia. *Our* bodies are not drawn out of this world, but our minds are. If that were not true, painting would be nothing but crude photography. Those thirty thousand-year-old cave paintings from Lascaux, France, are not crude copies of running animals; they are signs of archetypal animals. They are far more real, more alive, than photographs. They leap off the wall at you. They are pictures not of animals but of Animality. A Platonist painted them.

Some poetry does that: the words of the Koran to a Muslim, and of the Psalms to a Jew, and of the Gospels to a Christian, of the *Dhammapada* to a Buddhist and of the *Tao Te Ching* to a Taoist. They are not just wise and true, they are magical and powerful; like a beautiful woman, they turn our souls to butter. They are sacramental: they enact what they signify. They have not just meaning but *te*, spiritual power.

Some stories and plays have the power to literally haunt us, like ghosts: Hamlet, of course (because the whole play is a kind a haunting ghost), and *Oedipus Rex*, and Thornton Wilder's *Our Town*, which sent hard-hearted Hollywood audiences into uncontrollable tears, and George Macdonald's "The Golden Key," the best of all fairy tales according to Tolkien, and Tolkien's own *Lord of the Rings*, "which made one 12-year-old girl weep for two whole days, and his creation epic in *The Silmarillion*, which is even more beautiful, and H. G. Wells's story "The Door in the Wall, which haunts us because it says exactly what this lecture says— that there is a literal magic door in the wall of the world, but without Wells quite believing it. And even Beckett's *Waiting for Godot*, which could have been written by Socrates, Buddha, and Jesus in hilarious collaboration as the world's greatest joke: a world without *Logos*, a tower of babble.

Some *buildings* are doors in the wall. The Gothic cathedrals of the Middle Ages are doors, and windows. They do not just *have* stained glass windows that reveal the light beyond, they *are* such windows. They are miracles. They take heavy stone and make it fly, like angels. And we fly with them. Those flying buttresses are rocket fins. Every time I see a picture of the cathedral of Notre Dame I am amazed that it's still there; on its launching pad: I expect it to take off like a rocket and go back to heaven where it came from. What accounts for these miracles? They were incredibly far ahead of their time technologically. What built them? Not merely things in this world. Something in the other world did it, *through* us, not *from* us. It was crazy divine love igniting crazy human love. It was fire from Heaven.

The artist in us responds to these things. Why? Is it an accident? Does this response tell us nothing about our real selves and our real destiny and our real world? This is a powerful clue. I mean our love of beauty, not just of prettiness and satisfaction and harmony, but a beauty the breaks our hearts. This is the profoundest compliment you can ever give to any kind of artist: "you break my heart." When our hearts are broken with a beauty that shatters us like lightning, this is a strong clue that the lightning really comes from above, as it seems to; and that therefore there *is* an above, a "more". These brief storms of living water give a life to our desert-like spirits, a life that we have never known before. How could these thunderstorms really come not from the sky but only from the ground?

It's not a proof. Art doesn't *prove* anything. But it sure does sing something. Why not believe the song?

Book 10 of Plato's *Republic* contains a surprisingly stupid view of art: that it's only an imitation of nature, and thus two steps removed from ultimate reality, from the Forms. Plato did not love artists, but artists love Plato. In fact, all great artists are Platonists in that they try to present to us something that is *closer* to the Forms than nature is. They don't imitate nature; they bypass nature and imitate the Forms. They make us see, if only vaguely and uncertainly, through a glass, darkly, something of the paradise of pure Forms lying behind the surface appearances of things. They are a kind of remembrance of Paradise Lost.

Some kind of Paradise Lost myth is present in all cultures. It seems to be a kind of collective memory. Remember, in Greek mythology it was the goddess of memory who was the mother of the Muses, the nine inspiring goddesses of all art. In the ancient myths everything in the world we see carries a faint imprint or memory of a world that we do not see; and every hunter and weaver and healer and carver, every practical artist as well as every fine artist, imitates some Archetype, usually concretized in Ancestor.

Great art is not only a memory of Paradise Lost but also an anticipation of Paradise Regained; a hint, a hope, an appetizer, of future bliss. The world is like a scrim, a thin semi-transparent screen between the audience and the unseen reality behind the screen. And the artist knows how to light up that screen and show us those imprints. Great artists are like prophets, mediating between two worlds.

And the artist does this not only with beauty but also with ugliness, especially the beautiful ugliness that is tragedy, our highest and most beautiful narrative form. There are parallels in the other arts. Music in a minor key can move us more than music in a major key. And the more darkness a painter shows us, the more his light strikes us. For instance, the painting called "The Last Conversation" pictures Jesus and the Thief on the Cross dying together, descending into the darkness, and the central word in that conversation, the very last word, was the word "Paradise."

A seventh door through the walls of the cave is in the stuff of the cave itself, in the power of nature to make us happy. The cave is not just our motel room but our mother. We today insult her by calling her simply "the universe," but we used to call her Mother Nature, and we used to listen to her songs. She makes us happy by her songs. Why? Have you ever wondered that? Why do stars, oceans, lakes, rivers, trees, mountains, and deserts make us deeply happy? We can't live in them. We're not birds or fish or monkeys. We can't eat them. To use them we have to destroy them, like chopping down trees or damming rivers. But we love these things. We pay big bucks to see them, and vacation among them, and buy property near them. What mystical sugar did the Creator put into these things?

The Iroquois have a word for it: *orenda*, the mysterious power in nature to draw us and make us happy and even wise. According to the *Tao Te Ching*, it's the *te* or spiritual power of the Tao, the Way of Nature, the Pattern or Form or *Logos* of Nature, which in turn manifests the ultimate Tao beyond nature. That's what has such power to make us wise and simple and happy. It's the same Tao, the same pattern, in three places: in ultimate reality, in nature, and in the wise human life—just as in Plato it's the same Form in these three places. It's the Form that unifies man and nature.

We sense that; we sense a secret to our own identity in nature because both have the same ultimate origin, like a long lost sister and brother meeting. It's what Dylan Thomas meant when he wrote "The force that through the green fuse drives the flower / Drives my green age. . . . the force that drives the water through the rocks / Drives my red blood." Plato wasn't that kind of mystical romanticist about nature, but what's common to his vision and the vision of Romanticism is that reality is far greater than appearances; that what we see in nature is just the beautiful scrim. The light comes through it, not from it.

There are other clues too, but most of them are rarer. But some of these rare clues are even more convincing, to those who do see them. For instance, there are mystics, and mystical experiences, in every culture. And the great mystics don't typically seem to be crazy. Was Buddha crazy? Was St. Theresa? Was Lao Tzu? Read them! If that's crazy, I'd like to be crazy, please.

There are also accounts in all cultures of meetings with gods and angels and spirits and ghosts, and many of them also do *not* sound like stories in the *National Enquirer*. Some of them have been investigated with great scientific precision and discipline by the Society for Psychical Research.

There is also the phenomenon of mental telepathy, which most ordinary people have at last a little of, as when you suddenly notice someone behind you looking at you. How do you do that?

And there are visions, visionary dreams, which abound in all cultures and most of which are very surprising and even countercultural, so they're not just culturally acquired dreams. And many of them check out; they are objectively verified. Most of these are religious visions, but not all. And many of the people who see these things also seem credible.

And there are out of body experiences—literally millions of them, for today these are far more common than ever before because of CPR, and these experiences are impressively similar all over the world and all over the spectrum of people's religious beliefs and expectations. They do not come from drugs. And they change people's lives: everyone who has them gets suddenly wise and discover the same new value philosophy: that there are only two things in life that matter, love and truth. And they all suddenly and totally lose the strongest fear in life, the fear of death for the rest of their lives. It takes more faith to disbelieve in all these clues than to believe: it takes the faith that someday we will explain them all away by the sciences of the cave. I don't have enough facts to be an unbeliever.

From the philosopher's point of view there's a lack of clarity and definition about what we see through these holes, what the world outside the cave is composed of, what this Platonic realm means. Evidently, it is something more than abstract and static Platonic Forms (which themselves are much more than mere class concepts, remember). Platonic Forms are just the road map of the country outside the cave, so to speak. And Plato himself knew that Plato was not just a rationalist but also a mystic, and therefore a mythmaker, because he knew that we needed both *mythos*, concrete sacred story, and *Logos*, abstract rational understanding; that's why he ended all his most important dialogs with myths after he went as far as he could with reason. In fact, most of the world's great teachers, including Jesus, Buddha, and Lao Tzu, taught in parables and analogies more than in definitions and arguments. Because they all realized the Hamlet principle, that there's more in heaven and earth, that is, in reality, than in our philosophies, that is, in our minds. Only a few drops of the ocean can fit into a thimble.

The walls of the cave are teeming with holes, and some of them are not just windows to look through but doors wide enough to walk through. We can actually choose to live the life outside the cave, even though we don't fully understand it. What do I mean by that? I mean that the widest and most open door of all is the saints. Anyone can be one. All it takes is the will, the love.

Saints are even more convincing than mystics, because they *live*, not just *see*, the other world. They are people who love you not merely a little more than most people do; they are people who have a whole other *kind* of love, a love that is totally self-forgetful, totally fearless of death and pain and suffering and sacrifice, a love that seems to come down from heaven to earth and be willing to go down even more, from earth to death and hell for you. Christians say that you can see the light of Christ shining through the saints, and that light is absolute love.

The only force that can resist that love is the force that comes not from earth or nature but from darkness and evil: egotism and jealousy and envy and resentment at goodness. That's why saints are the most controversial people in the world. They're not nice. They're like light; they scare the bugs away.

But they're the most important clue because they tell us what we're all supposed to be. One of their followers once wrote: "Life contains only one tragedy, in the end: not to have been a saint." (Leon Bloy)

They're also the most wide-open door because even though not everyone can be a mystic, anyone can be a saint. One of them once wrote: "If you consult your own heart in all honesty you will be forced to see that there is one and only one reason why you are not as saintly as the early Christians: because you do not wholly want to be." (William Law)

Saints are wonderfully simple, like Platonic Forms or angels.

Plato was not a saint. But Socrates was. Erasmus wrote, "Saint Socrates, pray for us." I second the motion.

Socrates was also a martyr. How do you argue with a martyr? How do you argue with something stronger than the fear of death, and thus a powerful clue to something stronger than death? Socrates's arguments are great, but his example is more unanswerable than his arguments. When I read the *Phaedo*, I am not satisfied or convinced by Socrates's three philosophical arguments for the soul's immortality, profound as they are. But I am totally convinced by Socrates's death. He is like a Platonic Idea, like a god: unchangeable. Even death does not change him, but only brings out more clearly what is already in him. If you want to be convinced that there is a world outside the cave, if you want to be convinced that there is a world after death, if you want to be convinced of the soul's immortality, read Socrates's death scene in the *Phaedo*. When the idea of death and the idea of Socrates thus meet in your mind, it is the idea of death that will be changed, not the idea of Socrates.

Just as Buddhism is only the explanation in words for Buddha, and just as Christian philosophy and theology is only the explanation in words for Christ, so Platonism is only the explanation in words for Socrates. None of these three men—the three most influential men who ever lived—ever published a word. They did not have to. Why? For the same reason. When God showed Moses who He was, in the burning bush, He did not have to add any words to "I AM."

Meet these three men. They will change your life more than anyone else ever did, just as they changed history more than anyone else ever did. And the dialogs of Plato are the very best place to start.

I conclude with a kind of parable.

Let us say that you are a modernist and I am a Platonist. You and I walk along the same stone wall every day. It curves to the left at the next corner. Neither of us is absolutely certain that when we turn that corner we will not meet a homicidal maniac leaping over the wall to attack us. But you are also absolutely certain that when you turn that corner you will not meet an angel walking through that wall. And I am not certain of that. Which of us is to be envied and which of us is to be pitied?